BLUEPRINTS

For Generations

Ross Kellogg

Word Paint Publishing

Blueprints for Generations
Word Paint Publishing
Copyright © 2024 Ross Kellogg
All rights reserved

ISBN - 9798303671218

Cover design by: Ross Kellogg Word Paint Publishing
Library of Congress Control Number: 1CH12803V3

CONTENTS

Title Page	
Dedication	1
Preface	2
Intro	7
Part 1	9
Relationship	10
What are we teaching?	12
Starting right	14
Why discipline?	16
Part 2	19
A child is a nation	20
Parenting how God parents	24
Part 3	29
The principle of giving out of poverty	30
We must be healed first	34
Relationship above calling	40
The power of words	45

The skill of how to think	48
Delayed gratification	54
Be thankful - and resilient!	62
Put others first	67
Emotional control	72
Discipline out of love	78
Consequences	83
Prioritize True beauty	90
Teach Godly authority	97
No is a good word	101
Self-control	105
Feed them healthy food	109
The riches of an imaginative mind	113
Deal with it	118
The riches of purpose	123
Part 4	129
On the lookout	130
Warning signs	136
Part 5	138
Navigating Risk	139
The art of reason	142
Launch pad into adulthood	148
Ever growing Boundaries	150
Afterword	156

DEDICATION

This book is dedicated to my daughters Ruth and Naomi. Without you, life would have been void of the vibrant color, joy, love, laughter and insight that you bring wherever you go. Because of you I know the love of a father, and consequently, have come to know the Heavenly Father in a light I never otherwise would have. I love you and am forever thankful for you.

- Love Dad

PREFACE

I want to begin this book by simply stating the truth that there are no perfect mothers or fathers on earth. Every one of us who are endeavoring to parent both physical and spiritual children will make mistakes and fall short to be and provide everything that our kids need. God knows this! This is a beautiful part of His design which keeps all of us from worshiping the imperfect creation and draws our gaze and hearts to the perfect Father. The Lord is not looking for perfect people, He is looking for people who are humble and teachable with hearts that are fully committed to Him (*2 Chron 16:9*).

As I have taken time to gather these principles and pieces of wisdom on parenting I have been consistently and increasingly aware of my own shortcomings as a father, but just as glaringly have I felt His pleasure over my heart's yearning to grow in fatherhood. This is my desire for everyone reading this book. As we see ways to better our own parenting, we must recognize that condemnation, shame and regret are tools of the enemy and have no place in our lives. The Father is pleased with hearts that long to follow Him and walk in His ways, and our attention must remain focused on this truth; *He is infinitely more pleased in our choice to get up and follow Him than He is displeased with our failures.* He loves us!

This book is by no means an attempt to brag about my parenting, or to point fingers at those who don't parent by these same ideals. Rather, the goal of these writings is to share what I have learned through trial and error in my own life, and what I believe is insight gained through receiving correction from our heavenly Father as He has brought me back to His side time and time again to raise me up as a spiritual child into maturity. I believe this is His desire to do for all of us, and I am still in the middle of this journey.

Additionally, as I have seen and recognized my failures, I have also felt the Lord settling me deeper and deeper into the warmth of the His grace and love. He knows all of our imperfections and loves our children exponentially more than we can know. He holds them in His hands and will move in their lives regardless of our mistakes and personal shortcomings. I've heard it said that it is good to look back on our lives, *but don't stare*. We all would do some things differently if we could return and try again, but the Lord is never pointing at our failures in order to make us feel bad. He desires that we see what went wrong in the past so we can do it better next time, but even more than that *He wants us looking at Him* so we can be changed into His image, the best parent imaginable!

I am reminded that praying for our children avails as much, if not more, than the lessons we teach them as they grow. This isn't to diminish the importance of what we teach them, but to magnify the power of a parent who lifts their children up to the true Father in prayer! None of us have done parenting perfectly and no one ever will here on earth. This is why seeking God's grace and then turning around and giving it out to others is so essential; we can't have true relationship with the Lord or others without a continuous inflow and outflow of His grace and forgiveness.

This book has been written with the bold and open call to live an intentional life with the purpose of building our generation's house so that the ceiling above us will be the floor for those after us to build upon. As we grow and learn to walk closer to the Lord, we are continuously changed into His image. The mistakes we make in our lives become lessons for those coming after us to learn from, so that our pitfalls and errors are replicated by neither our physical nor spiritual children.

In the book of Exodus, we see that we are called to honor our fathers and mothers so that it will go well for us. One way we do this is by learning from both their successes as well as their mistakes, and resolving to not only do it better, but to encourage *our* children to take what they've learned from us and go even farther!

So often we see people who continue to live in the broken-down shambles of a house that fell apart generations ago, unaware that life can be different and that they can be the starting point for a whole new family tree. Most people have begun and continued to live their entire lives with neither the tools nor the knowledge to build a new home for the ones who will come after them. Not only is it possible, but one of our most basic callings is to lay a foundation that is sturdy enough to build generation after generation upon. The purpose of this book is not only to declare that it can be done, but to also highlight truths and lessons on how to do it!

It has been said that children don't come with an instruction manual, and while that is true to an extent, the greater truth to grasp is that the Lord has given us all we need to know so that we can raise children into Godly leaders who will pioneer a path into the Father's Kingdom for theirs and future generations.

2 Peter 1:3 tells us that *"His divine power has granted us all things that pertain to life and godliness."* The wisdom that we find in the Word of God as well as in the words of those who have gone

before us provide us with priceless insights into how we approach this immense calling of being a parent.

No matter how you were raised, what you have gone through, or how badly you may have messed up, you have the incredible opportunity to change the course of not only your life, but every life that God has brought into your care. You can completely reverse negative cycles that you have received or have led others into, and your family tree can grow in a new and life-giving direction from here on!

The people of our nation, *and indeed the world*, have become more and more deeply mired in a society and culture of fatherlessness, which has actually sent them on a desperate quest for identity and ultimately (*even unknowingly*) on a search for the Father Himself. The glaring truth is that the answer they seek is wholly found in a God who loves them beyond their wildest imagination. He is offering everyone a path to Righteousness, Peace, and Joy, and *it is up to us* to lead them in how to walk in it!

INTRO

Being born is the beginning. This holds true both physically as well as spiritually, and one of the most overlooked parts of being *born again* is the need to be *raised again*. Paul refers to this process in Romans 12:2 by telling us, *"Do not conform to the pattern of this world, but be transformed by the renewing of your mind. Then you will be able to test and approve what God's will is…"*

The pattern of this world is the way that the flesh thinks. This is how things are done in the mind of man and the wisdom of the world, which are both outside of God's will. We must have our minds renewed so that we can distinguish between what is God's will and what is just a tradition, a cultural norm, or a straight up destructive cycle that we have unwittingly been in, sometimes for generations!

The purpose of this book is not only for parents who desire to raise their children wisely, but it is for every one of us who desire to see

God as our true Father and to have our minds renewed in this light. This has been written using spiritual principles that not only apply to us parenting physical and spiritual children but also can be applied in relation to how our heavenly Father parents us. Negative patterns that we find ourselves in can often be traced back to their origins which began in our own childhood, either through gaps in our earthly fathers' parenting, or our personal resistance to receive it. Recognizing our own lack allows us to approach the Father as His children so that we can present our need to Him and receive His perfect, restorative guidance.

It is never too late to be parented by the true Father. In fact, this is our calling to walk in for the rest of our earthly lives, *to know Him as* the Father! God doesn't cease being our Dad when we become adults, rather, true relationship with Him only leads to a greater and greater increase of this reality throughout our entire time on earth and into eternity.

This book is intended to be first applied to ourselves, and then extended to our children, both spiritual as well as physical.

PART 1

The God of Relationship

RELATIONSHIP

God is the God of relationship! Relationship is at the center of every meaningful and worthwhile aspect of life and is one of the most valuable things that we can take with us into eternity. Relationship permeates the foundation of every facet that society is built upon.

The health of every community will depend wholly on the health of the relationships within it. Without relationship with God there is only dead religion. Without relationship in a marriage there is only a contract. How often does a relationship between two people who care deeply for each other dwindle into a business partnership, or a begrudging roommate, or worst of all, lifelong adversaries?

Without healthy relationship in family there develops a cold, antiseptic environment that will inevitably create a breeding ground for wounds that can send a soul careening into a life of brokenness and shipwreck. In God's Word, and throughout history, we see an incredible truth; *the seeds we plant in our lifetime (even if we don't personally live to see their fruit) will grow and impact generations to come, and can even dictate the destiny of an entire people group!*

This incredible truth works on both a positive and a negative level, depending on what is sown into the soil. Seeds of love, purpose, and Godly relationship will breed people who change the world around them for God's Kingdom. Conversely, seeds of neglect, selfishness and wounding will also find soil to grow and replicate their bitter fruit. What we plant now will be growing and producing fruit for generations to come! Are you planting carelessly or with intention?

WHAT ARE WE TEACHING?

As a society, we devote the majority of our children's lives to education, but what are they spending all this time learning? What are they being taught in those facilities, hour after hour, day after day? Healthy relationship built on the Father's truth is the most important aspect of every individual's life, but how much time is spent teaching young people how to interact in a friendship? In a romantic relationship? Towards authority? In conflict? The list goes on, but the truth of the matter is that *most relational learning is not done intentionally but rather unwittingly.*

Most people learn to interact with one another either by mirroring the actions of those before them, or by reckless trial and error. This inevitably leads to a downward generational cycle called *"The tyranny of the familiar,"* which is the tendency of a person to stay in, or gravitate back towards, the environment they are most familiar with. This explains why women who grew up with an alcoholic or abusive father routinely end up marrying an alcoholic or abusive husband. Men who grew up with a controlling mother end up marrying a manipulative wife. Children who aren't taught to make decisions based on truth, but rather on emotional autopilot, will eventually slide back into the rut that they are most familiar with.

We must prioritize teaching truth that matters! What is the benefit if we raise a child who is adept at math but crushes the hearts of those closest to him? Who cares that a person is a "straight A" student if she is unable to control her temper? *What does it profit a man to gain the entire world but lose his soul?* It is time to shift our focus from teaching children how to ace a test, work a career, and plan for retirement, and begin to turn our eyes to raising sons and daughters who know their true identity that the Father has given them. It is time to stop chasing our own dreams and desires and realize that our lives are meant to be invested into the lives of the next generation.

These young people are ones who are desperately searching for meaning, searching for fathers and mothers, and ultimately for a God who deeply loves them. This is our calling from the Father; are you willing to give up your life so that others can receive the true and incredible life that He has for them? As Jesus said in John 15:13, *"Greater love has no man than this, to lay down his life for His friends."*

STARTING RIGHT

The Song of Solomon is a book in the bible that, throughout history, has been largely left alone by Christians. On the seldom times when it is opened, this book is usually referred to as an allegory of Christ and the Church. Because of the incredible depth and dimension of the Word of God, this *is* true, but it is not the primary purpose that this book was written.

The Song of Solomon is a true history written by King Solomon, the richest and wisest king in history, and is a love story about he and his wife. It tells of how they were both raised well (*one of them in an unconventional family*), prepared themselves for marriage, and modeled a godly relationship through good and difficult times. It shows how they courted, married, had healthy intimacy, close conflict, godly resolution, and ultimately a vibrant life together. This is not a marriage of kings' alliances or of political strategies; this is a story about love and commitment that begins, grows, and is wisely stewarded between two people.

The desire and purpose of Blueprints is to identify principles for raising children into godly men and women using principles and wisdom found all throughout God's Word. This book is the beginning of a series of books which will take a larger look at relationships in general, but it all begins *(as it always does)* with how a child is raised.

WHY DISCIPLINE?

What is the point of discipline? It's difficult, painful, and almost always leans in the opposite direction of how we feel in the moment. Is it worth it? Is it really that important? In the book of 1 Samuel Chapter Two we find a story about a priest named Eli who has sons that are serving in the temple under his leadership.

The Bible describes Eli's sons as *"worthless men."* This is an extremely bold description coming from God! These men would steal people's sacrifices that they had brought to the Lord, bully and threaten those who resisted them, and even sleep with young women who came to serve in the Temple! Everybody saw what was going on, yet nothing was done.

We get some insight into Eli's parenting techniques when he finally confronts his sons for doing things that the Bible calls a *"very great sin in the eyes of the Lord"* (1 Sam 2:17). Eli gives them a verbal warning! His sons were probably a couple decades past any effect that a verbal warning could have had on them, and yet that's as far as Eli takes it. Do you think that these men were model citizens up until that point when they took a turn for the worse and decided to steal someone's sacrifice? Absolutely not. This was a life-long pattern of weak fatherhood and parenting that Eli had lived in, walked in, and ultimately led his children down.

Parents can't be blamed for all of their children's poor choices, but that doesn't alleviate the responsibility of a parent to influence, impact, and lead their child down the path of life. Proverbs 23:13-14 illustrates this truth by telling us, *"Do not withhold discipline from a child; if you strike him with a rod he will not die. If you strike him with a rod, it will save his soul from death."*

By withholding discipline from his sons, Eli not only exposed the people of Israel to corruption and sin but he also set his own sons up for painful consequences which would end up coming from the Lord Himself.

Children have free will, and we cannot hold parents to account for all of their kids' decisions, but the truth is that we as parents have the opportunity to influence their choices *by leading them into discipline*, and the refusal to do so clearly sets them up for failure.

The caveat this brings, however, is that in

order for us to lead our children into discipline, we as parents must first receive it in our own lives. Few things are more miserable than a person who preaches what they don't live. Children can spot a phony from a mile away, *so get ready to walk out what you are teaching!*

PART 2

God's Perspective

A CHILD IS A NATION

Genesis 25:23 – *"And the Lord said to her, 'Two nations are in your womb, and two peoples from within you shall be divided; the one shall be stronger than the other, the older shall serve the younger."*

How can an entire nation fit inside of a womb? To God, a child represents something so much more than just a single life. When we step back from our limited viewpoint and look from God's perspective, we begin to understand how the Lord sees beyond just one generation, beyond just one person. When the Father looks at an individual, He is not just seeing the single human before Him, He sees the seed from which hundreds, thousands, even millions of people will come!

God pours into us with this in mind, and He is expecting that what He teaches us will become a part of who we are, and thereby be infused into the next generation of each person that comes under both our physical and spiritual parenthood. *When God sees a child, He sees a nation*, and how we invest in this person will end up specifically raising, teaching and discipling the multitudes that will come through them.

This, however, is a double-edged sword and applies to both the positive as well as the negative investments that are made in these little ones. God is a God of family. The first line of the Lord's prayer begins with "Our Father," which automatically denotes the idea that we are brothers and sisters in His Kingdom. It doesn't matter if you are married or single, have children or no children, young or old. If you have been born again through Jesus, then you are a part of a family for eternity! Because of this you have the incredible honor *and* responsibility of walking with Him while raising up sons and daughters to do the same.

As the saying goes, "*It is easier to build strong children than to repair broken people*." While the principle is true, it would probably be better said that it takes *less time* to build strong children than to repair broken people, because when it comes to raising children, *"easy"* is rarely a word that applies!

Sadly, most children are not raised but simply allowed to grow up under the same roof as their parents. That is to say, most parents approach family life by putting their focus on their own goals and desires while, at times, bringing the children along for the ride. This usually partners with the belief that the responsibility of the parent in raising children is merely to offer them provision for the basic needs of life, namely food and shelter.

Although provision is an important aspect of parenthood, and noble in intent, this mentality results in a child growing up with physical nourishment and protection from the elements while never receiving the most crucial aspects of family; the relational and spiritual tools to navigate their way through life. Incidentally, not only is the passing down of these tools the parent's most important job, but it is in teaching them that we find some of the greatest joys of life, both for the child as well as the parent.

Neglecting to fulfill this crucial role as a parent not only causes a missed opportunity for love and fulfilment on both sides, but results in raising a son or daughter who lacks crucial spiritual, relational, and emotional skills necessary to build and foster true, healthy relationships.

It is not a dishonor to our parents when we recognize their failures in order to improve upon them, rather it is a tribute that we make to them by taking their torch farther than they were able to. The ceiling of their life must become the floor upon which we build ours, and likewise our ceiling to those who come after us. Rather than traveling in the well-trodden ruts of our parents and culture, we must begin to purposefully cut and pave new roads in order to intentionally prepare our children for life. We base this on how the Lord parents us.

PARENTING HOW GOD PARENTS

Do you know God as your Father? Some may know Him as their Savior, Provider, Healer and Comforter, but our potential to walk with Him in the fullness that He has called us into will not be complete until we know Him as our Father.

There is a line in a song that paints a vivid picture of a common stance people unknowingly take towards their mother or father who, in some capacity, hurt or disappointed them; *"I'm still angry at my parents for what their parents did to them."* This is such a true and vivid picture of the futility of blaming others, especially someone who is as close to us as our parents are. This is, however, the ditch that a majority of people find themselves in.

Why is it that, when so many are questioned about their bitterness, insecurities, failures and woundings, their answers almost always lead back to one source: their parents? How many people have sworn to never be like their father or mother, only to end up wearing the same shoes, walking the same paths, and causing the same woundings as they did? Without forgiving and honoring our parents, we are doomed to receive and be bound up by the same generational curses as they were.

The greatest reason people fail as parents is not because their parents failed them, *it is because they failed to forgive their parents*, and thus failed to know God rightly as their true Father. 2 Corinthians 3:18 teaches us the principle that *we become like what we behold.*

Only when we truly see and get to know our heavenly Father will we begin to rightly understand and walk in parenthood. This gives us the ability to see the failures of our own parents as a wrong turn that they took at a fork in the road that we also will eventually come to. This then enables us to see them rightly, which will open the blinds in our hearts to steer around the problems that they fell into. Once we see them as fallible humans who also had parents that made mistakes raising them, then we will be able to stop the negative cycles and begin a new line of blessing for the next generation.

Only through truly knowing the Father's love and forgiveness are we able to forgive those who failed us in times when we needed them the most, and thereby learn and grow from those failures. Solely when we see through the eyes of forgiveness will we be set free to pioneer a new path of parenthood that will end the destructive patterns that have continued in our lineage, sometimes for centuries! It is only then that we are able to start a new heritage which will bless families for generations to come.

Some *(but not all)* of what are called "generational curses" are merely patterns of wrong thinking, selfish habits, or unconquered flesh. Many of the problems we face as adults are simply immature childish habits that we were never led to overcome through humility and self-discipline in our childhood. It is imperative to recognize that the responsibility to master and change these issues in our lives has shifted off of our parents *(mentors, role models, etc…)* and rests now entirely on us. *If you don't change where you are going, you will end up where you are headed.*

2 Timothy 1:7 tells us, "we haven't been given a spirit of fear but of power, love and self-discipline." If we could accomplish everything with only power or love, why would we be given a spirit of self-discipline? Do you know what the word disciple simply means "disciplined one?" Paul says in Philippians 3:14, *"I can do all things through Him who strengthens me."* We must learn to partner with the Lord in His work so that we are able to walk in step with Him in accomplishing His

purposes in our lives *(Galatians 5:25)*.

When we look at how the Father approaches relationship with His children, we find that His discipline and love are inseparable. Hebrews 12:5 reveals this to us; *"Have you forgotten the exhortation that addresses you as sons? 'My son do not regard lightly the discipline of the Lord, nor be weary when you are reproved by Him. For the Lord disciplines those He loves and chastises every son whom He receives.'"* True Godly discipline is to be greatly desired because, as we see in this verse, it is sure evidence of a parent who loves their child. This leads us to the principle that a healthy relationship between a parent and their child cannot exist without discipline.

Progress is rarely made on accident, and we only have victory over lifelong negative cycles by the power of the Holy Spirit combined with our disciplined participation. Many try one without the other and inevitably end in failure. The Holy Spirit is called "*the Helper*," not "*the doer*." Some people make the claim that *"it wasn't me; it was all God!"* While this is a noble effort to give God the glory it is ultimately not true. If God wanted to do it Himself He absolutely could. Instead, He chooses to invite us into partnership with Him in order to accomplish His purposes, thus He chooses to make *our willing involvement necessary in order for Him to move*.

It is true that without Him no eternal work in our lives would be possible, (*and He is accomplishing eternally more than we see or know about*) but without us cooperating much of it won't happen! What an honor the Lord has given us: to partner with Him in His work here on earth!

PART 3

Principles of Parenting

THE PRINCIPLE OF GIVING OUT OF POVERTY

In the book of Mark, Chapter Twelve, Jesus points out to His disciples a money box which people were putting their tithes and offerings into. As they watched people putting in large sums of money, there came a widow who dropped in two small copper coins. After seeing this, Jesus declared that she had given more than any of the others, because they had given out of their abundance, but she had given out of her poverty.

Did Jesus minimize the giving of those who contributed out of their abundance? Absolutely not. Their giving was appreciated and necessary for use in the temple. What the Lord did was to magnify this woman's heart position, which was the key to the impact of her gift. Jesus wasn't claiming powerlessness of giving out of abundance, but rather the incredible power of giving out of one's poverty!

There are certain skills and strengths that each of us have received from our parents (*or those in authority over us*) which the Lord is pleased to see us operate in and give out of. However, no matter how many areas of abundance we have been gifted in, we all have compartments in our lives that we were not taught or equipped to be successful in. These places which lacked parental investment create gaps in our leadership that, if not filled, become recurring voids or even curses that are passed on to the next generation. So how do we reverse these cycles?

In Galatians Chapter Two, Paul tells us that it is no longer he who lives, but Christ who lives in Him. When we submit to the Lord, He lives in and operates through us. Were you without a father growing up? Come to the true Father. He will teach you what it is to be a parent, and as you walk with Him in submission to His Holy Spirit, He will not only give you the resources that you need to be a parent, but *He will parent through you!* Did you have no one to lead you through the most impressionable and vulnerable times in your life, times when you most needed a leader? Come to the true Leader and He will make you a guide for those in the same need you were also once in.

Growing up in the country, my family had several horses, one being named Rebel, who's name by no means reflected his character. This was the slowest, oldest, most predictable horse I have ever known. I always assumed that he was lazy, but looking back I now think that in those days he was just a couple of breaths away from the grave, and he knew it. Not only was this horse never in a hurry, but I don't think he even had the capacity to be in a hurry.

One afternoon when I was five, my sister and I went for a ride on old Rebel to visit a neighbor up the road. Being that Rachel was a few years older than I, she took the reins while I just held on to the back of the saddle and enjoyed the view. As we plodded our way up the dirt road my sister noticed a white van driving down the hill towards us. Thinking nothing of it, she continued to urge Rebel to not fall asleep as he walked, while I stared at the gravel going by inch after inch.

Just then, the white van sped by and suddenly slammed on the brakes, skidding to a stop about thirty yards behind our horse. I watched the scene unfold with detached fascination as a dirty looking man jumped out of the passenger side door and began sprinting in our direction. I was vaguely aware of panic rising in my sister and spreading towards me as this wild looking individual quickly closed the gap between us. Rachel desperately kicked Rebel's ribs in an attempt to make him run for what would probably be the first time in decades.

Slowly Rebel began to trot. The man was mere yards away at this point, and I just remember burying my face in my sister's back as I anticipated the filthy hands of this nutcase grabbing my leg in the next couple of seconds. At that instant Rebel broke into a full-blown run, pulling easily away from our pursuer at the last possible moment, quickly leaving him in the dust.

I will never forget the relief that we both felt as Rebel carried us safely away from an unknown yet definitely undesirable outcome. As long as we owned him, that horse had zero energy, strength, or even will to run, but in the moment that we needed him, I believe the Lord came down and filled him with whatever it took to save our lives. That horse gave out of his poverty that day.

What were you lacking most when you were too young to provide it for yourself? The Lord desires to first fulfill this need in your heart, and then, through you, He will be to others the fulfillment of that same need. Come to Him! In doing so, He will equip you to offer to others that which you were always missing. This is truly giving out of your poverty, and this kind of offering is worth exponentially more and will reach infinitely farther than any gift given out of abundance.

WE MUST BE HEALED FIRST

There is a story that took place in the late 1800's of a child raised by two parents who were both hearing impaired. The child could hear perfectly and was very intelligent, however, growing up, he was only taught to communicate through sign language. When he was eventually introduced to other children, they encountered a huge shock; this bright young man didn't know how to speak! Over time and with effort he learned how to verbally communicate and eventually lived a full life, becoming a good husband and father who was well respected in the community, but was always known as a man of few words.

The parallels are clear. It's said, *"we don't see the world as it is, but we see the world as we are."* The correlations between a physical disability and a spiritual or emotional wounding are extremely similar. It is normal and right for parents to approach their child in the way that they themselves would like to be approached, and to teach their children from the same angle they themselves would learn from. The problem arises, however, when the parent raises their child through the filter of their own unhealed wound.

A person, for example, who has been wounded by rejection will tend to desire continuous reassurance or approval from others. They seek over-clarification to ensure any words spoken are not a reopening of that wound, or a sign of possible future wounding. Someone with this wounding generally lives with a vague anticipation that their relationships will have a short life span, and they may opt to leave the relationship first if they see any signs of the other faltering. Operating under the false spirit of suspicion rather than true discernment, they constantly question the motives of others, often accusing people of the things they are most afraid of. It is common for people influenced by this spirit to be overly cautious in team settings, afraid to step on toes or offend those around them through normal interactions. Desiring to be treated in excessive gentleness, they misinterpret anything else as unkind or even abusive.

Imagine raising a child in this environment. This child will grow to not only approach the world from a skewed view, but they will unreasonably expect the world to treat them in the same way their wounded parent desired *(or demanded)* to be treated. They would believe that the rest of the world is guilty of the false accusations their parents leveled at it, and would also believe that other people who don't treat them with the same care that a wounded person should be treated are actually being hurtful. This is called a *phantom wound*.

This leads to what is called a *"self-fulfilling prophecy."* Since most people desire to live in a world that makes sense, they tend to push others away who act irrationally, and since unseen wounds aren't rational, people who carry them tend to be further rejected, thereby fulfilling their own fears of rejection. Living and raising others to walk throughout their lives with unhealed or *phantom wounds* will end up creating real wounds in both those who carry this baggage as well as in others.

One afternoon, when our daughters Ruth and Naomi were seven and eight years old, we decided to go for a long walk together. At this time, we were living outside of town in a farmhouse surrounded by orchards, which were in turn surrounded by roads and different scatterings of public land with many roads and trails to walk and explore. There was a three-mile loop right out our back door that I would take when I went running, and so that day we decided to take this little trek together as a family.

Once we had gotten far enough into the hills that we were out of the orchards and away from houses, I decided to give the girls a little challenge. I told them that, while their mother and I walked the path around the base of the hill, they should walk over the top of it and meet us on the other side. This seemed like a safe little adventure that they could take together which would bolster their confidence while also exercising some of their independence.

Naomi assured us all that she understood the plan and would lead Ruth over the hill to our meeting spot, so we all set off. Folake and I walked quickly in order to arrive before the girls did so they could see us from far off and prevent any confusion, but after nearly twenty minutes of waiting I knew that something was up and decided to hike up the knoll and meet them halfway.

As I crested the top of the hill, I had a tinge of panic when I looked in every direction and found that they were nowhere in sight. I hiked all the way down the incline and back to where we had started with still no sign of them. I then raced back up and over to where Folake still waited, and then back up the slope once again, scouring the hillside for any glimpse of a brightly colored jacket or sweatshirt. Nothing.

As I stared out at the horizon praying for

God's intervention, I noticed movement a couple miles away. Clear out in the distance I saw two little girls holding hands and walking in the opposite direction. I called for them, but they were out of earshot, and so I set off at a jog to close the distance to a point where they would be able to hear me. Soon, drawing close enough that they could finally hear my screams, they turned around and came racing back, collapsing into my arms in a pile of tears and relief.

What had happened, it turned out, was that Naomi hadn't been paying as much attention as she let on during my instructions, and after walking a few paces up the hill, had turned and set off in the direction which felt the most right to her. After discovering they were lost, they had already begun formulating a plan on how to survive from here on without parents, and had fully accepted their new life as orphans.

Wounding skews our inner compass, and if we head out on an incorrect trajectory based on a mistaken directional reading, we will lead others down the wrong path. Does this mean that we all have to be perfectly healed and well before we enter into community or friendships? Of course not. Actually, community is a key component that we need in order to see our blind spots. Every one of us are a work in progress. The Lord is incredibly gracious and merciful towards us and calls us to be the same to each other. What is being highlighted here is the importance of recognizing areas in our lives that our own inner compass may have been skewed, tilting us onto a wrong trajectory. Have I approached areas of my life with a phantom wound? Do I have a real wound that is now creating a phantom wound in my child or those who look up to me? These are questions that we must bring to the Father.

Growing together in a healthy community is one of the primary ways we receive healing. The key is to be drawing closer to the Father and His people, walking in His light together, and continuously receiving His guidance and correction (*especially through each other*) so these wounds can be identified and healed. This is how we lead healthy, productive lives in the Kingdom, and prevent the passing on of generational wounds to our children.

Hosea 4:9, *"And what the priests do, the people also do…" (NLT)*

RELATIONSHIP ABOVE CALLING

Proverbs 24:27 tells us to *"prepare your work outside, get everything ready for yourself in the field, and after that, build your house."* This proverb speaks to the wisdom of thinking ahead, especially as a young person preparing for life. From the beginning, look out ahead and think where this path is leading. Is your life geared toward how much fun and how many memories you can make, or are you preparing to be a place of refuge for people who depend on you, who have no one else to look to? How common is it for people to have their sights set on love, romance, and personal goals, but when it all comes to them, are completely unprepared for the physical, emotional and spiritual responsibilities of taking care of another life?

God can redeem and bless anything no matter where it starts, as He has done in my own life, but the purpose of this book isn't to speak on how to launch haphazardly and then ask for God's forgiveness and blessing; rather it is to find and highlight the very best way to go about it from start to finish.

I begin this section in this way because it is better to prepare oneself beforehand to provide for the needs of others, so that when the family comes, focus and attention can then be shifted to the people who need it. In the beginning, righteousness appears to be bondage, but always ends in freedom, while sin takes the form of freedom but always ends in bondage. In the same way, preparing ourselves may have the appearance of drudgery, but results in much more freedom long term.

When our kids were still in their single digit ages, I worked outside the home while Folake stayed with them and homeschooled. My job at the time allowed for a four-day weekend every other week, but I still longed for more time with my wife and daughters. One morning, I had the taken the day off and Folake had plans in town, so as she was walking out the door she casually asked if I could homeschool the girls for the day. I said that I would and set a mental reminder to look over whatever work she had planned for them.

Although it was summertime and warm out, it began to rain, and as the water came down in torrents, I noticed a large muddy puddle beginning to accumulate on the back side of the house. As the morning wore on, the puddle grew until it resembled a small pond just outside our back door. When I could handle it no more, I finally declared to the girls that class was over but homeschool was just beginning! I told them to put on their swimsuits and we all proceeded out the back door and into the gigantic mud puddle. We spent the better part of the afternoon playing together in the rainy slop, while the girls completely caked themselves from head to toe in sticky, slimy mud. Even though I had to spray them off with cold hose water, they still declare to this day that their favorite memory of homeschooling was that homeschool day in the mud, and I would agree.

I have spent many days of my life working. Lots of those days were enjoyable while some were not, but the times I have spent with my family have outweighed any advancement, victory, or accomplishment that I have ever found in work.

Providing for the family is a real and important part of being a parent, and this part of parenthood cannot be overlooked or understated. *However*, this calling and privilege of being a provider is often so twisted and abused that it can turn from being a blessing over the family into actually being a curse that destroys relationships! How can this be?

There is an axiom describing how, for the

first half of every man's life he seeks security, and for the second half he seeks significance. Work is one of the easiest, most common, and yet ultimately least effective ways in which people do this. "*The principle of secondary truths*" speaks directly to this matter.

There are certain ideas that are only true as long as they don't overtake or eclipse other truths when it comes to priority or importance. For example, if you boil it all down, the biblical purpose of church is to be a house of prayer for all nations, while the purpose of church leadership is to equip the people of God for ministry, and each individual's ministry is to love God first and then others.

Now, it takes finances in order for the church to operate and accomplish these callings. This is a secondary truth, because while it is true that the church needs money to operate, the primary truths are those listed above. What would happen if that necessity for money suddenly became the driving factor of the church? What happens to churches that shift their focus from being a place of relationship with God to being a business that prioritizes and structures around making of profits and the accumulation of wealth? It becomes an empty shell of what it was meant to be, and although some good can still come out of it, ultimately it has lost its purpose and become a source of wounding and disillusionment. One truth must never be exalted to the exclusion of another.

A thing like work, which can have so much purpose and fulfilment, operates under the same principle. Work has the potential to be a great avenue of blessing, purpose, and even fulfilment, as long as it never becomes the source of those things. If relationship with the Lord, our spouse, or children ever begins to take a back seat to our time at the office, there is a problem. If our security or significance is sourced from anywhere but the Father Himself, then those secondary truths have now become lies.

Connect with the Lord, your spouse, and your children every day. Find ways to look them in the eyes and share something special with them that no one else gets from you. Do your work well and with excellence, *"as unto the Lord,"* but do your relationships even better! The people whom God has entrusted to you will carry the love and connection they receive from you for the rest of their lives, and even pass it on to others who will do the same. No one ever looks back and wishes they had spent more time away from their kids or loved ones, so take this into consideration as you are waking up every day, and be faithful with those whom God has given you!

THE POWER OF WORDS

My mom tells a story about when I was young, and she was struggling to lead me through certain issues in my life. It was during this particular period that I was acting out, breaking rules, and generally defying any kind of direction given to me by an authority figure. She had tried talking to me, spanking me, making me stand in the corner, and as many other types of punishment as she could think of, but I just continued on in my defiance.

One day, she noticed me doing something that wasn't quite noteworthy, but at least wasn't downright bad, and so she decided to come over and comment to me on it.

"Hey Ross," she said, "well done feeding the chickens today. You are really faithful at doing that chore."

She recollects that something in me

brightened just a bit that morning, and I wasn't quite as ornery as I had been on previous days. She decided to take note of and comment on as many positive things as she could find about me every day and see what happened. As it is, a difficult person or child tends to compel frustration rather than compliments, so the decision to speak and highlight positive things in their lives takes a high level of intentionality and self-control. My mother relates how she saw changes in me almost overnight, my attitude drastically changed, and over time my mom began to see significant improvement in my heart and actions. Every time my attitude began to sink my mother would go back to this method of speaking live over me, and it always bore fruit.

There is power in speaking life. Proverbs 18:21 tells us that *"the power of life and death are in the tongue."* The words that we speak will literally change the people around us. Our comments will frame someone's entire day, sometimes longer. Resolve to never speak negative comments about your children, but rather make up your mind to recognize and speak out true things about them as often as you can. These comments that you speak over your child are seeds of destiny that will take root in their hearts and bear fruit as they grow.

Do your comments sound like *"you always keep such a messy room,"* or *"you can be so selfish sometimes!"* or *"you are such a brat..."* If so, just remember, *kids believe what you tell them.* What if instead, about the same scenarios, you spoke life? For example, *"Clean up your room, because you are someone that takes care of your things,"* or *"You have a sharing heart and God wants to use you to bless others,"* or maybe, *"this attitude doesn't suit you, you are someone who has a heart for God."*

While I was backpacking through South America, I met a girl from Israel named Tali, a good friend whom my sister and I traveled with together through parts of Peru and Bolivia. One day she stopped me on the side of a busy street and asked if I wanted to play a game. Wary of her practical jokes, I was hesitant, but she assured me that it was good fun and began to explain the rules. You had sixty seconds to say all the nice things that you noticed about the other person, and afterwards they had the same amount of time to speak over you. I agreed, and to this day I still recall some of the caring and intentional words she spoke to me.

This interaction was so impactful that I have made a point to play the game throughout my life periodically with my family and those close to me. A simple sixty second game on the side of a busy street in Bolivia planted kindness in my soul that I have never forgotten. That is the power of words.

THE SKILL OF HOW TO THINK

One of the quickest and easiest ways to teach a subject to large groups of people is by giving them information and requiring them to memorize it. This manner of public education has unfortunately seeped into many facets of how we as a society tend to teach and learn. While information is essential, and the ability to memorize is crucial, the potential of the two will either lie dormant or be manipulated without *the ability to think*. The discernment for when and how to use the subject matter is the key that turns the lock.

In the summer of 1994, my family lived on the side of a mountain on a small homestead which bordered thousands of acres of public land. I was fourteen years old, had a motorbike, and the world was almost my oyster - I just wasn't quite able to pry it out of its shell yet.

During that summer my parents both

worked, and since my older sister was away at college, my parents begrudgingly left me to my own devices. This freedom, however, came at the price of a long list of chores that I was to accomplish each day before I was released to roam the countryside with a neighbor friend who also had a dirt bike.

One day, on the list of chores I found that morning, I saw that I was to build a fence across a couple hundred yards of our pastureland. Having dug countless fencepost holes in our rock laden soil for my dad before, I didn't think much of it, even though I had technically never before built a fence before on my own.

I got up early so I could beat the rising summer temperatures and be finished by the time my friend arrived, who was planning to bring up some Mountain Dew and a Jean-Claude Van Damme movie. I hoped to be done early enough that we would at least have time to do some karate in the barn before it got dark.

By the time my neighbor rolled in on his blue Kawasaki 175, I was just putting the finishing touches on my first fence. Little did I know that by the time I was done with it a week later, this would somehow end up being my fifth fence with only one fence ever having seen its way to completion.

We were halfway through our karate film when my dad burst through the door demanding that we shut the movie off and get back outside to finish the fence.

"I finished it an hour ago," I protested, seriously confused by his statement.

"It's not straight. Pull it up and do it right," he responded and left the room.

After having labored on that fence for most of the day, I was pretty disheartened, but I also knew better than to argue with my dad after he hit that level of intensity. We turned off the movie and spent the rest of the evening pulling up the fence.

The next day I again started early and went through the same process as the day before. This time, however, I stood at one end of the future fence line and held my thumb up in front of my eyes to try and give myself a good gauge of what a straight line should be.

"Good enough," I said. Once again, as I was finishing, my friend arrived with the VHS tape *(which still had another twenty-four hours left on the rental)* and we settled in to see how Van Damme would dish his next steaming bowl of rich, creamy justice. Once again, my dad arrived home and gave us the same undesired news; it was not good enough.

This pattern continued each day, costing my friend and I nearly three dollars in late fees as well as scores of hours of wasted labor, each day ending with the same result; it's not straight, do it again.

To this day, I'm not sure if my dad meant to teach me a lesson or if this project was just another failed test that he stamped as it came across his desk each night, but I learned one of the most important lessons of my life that summer. I learned how to figure it out. There are many ways to teach a kid how to think, to reason, and to figure out a solution, and this was far from the most efficient, but I will say that I learned something that day. I finally comprehended how to stop running into the same wall, to think through what was going wrong and to carve a path around it. Basically, I learned how to use a string line. Fence completed.

Vladimir Lenin, champion of communism, dictator of the Soviet Union and mass murderer of his own people, was a master in manipulation. In respect to young people who were being approached with the idea of communism, he referred to them as "*useful idiots.*" He reasoned that they were those who would hear an attractive idea which had a hint of truth and moral high ground and would embrace it wholeheartedly. They didn't possess the reasoning power to resist the momentum of the crowd or the deception of superficial morals. They thus became tools for misdirection and subterfuge who Lennon used to spread the great tragedy of communism and ultimately enslave an entire empire of people.

Our goal in teaching our children isn't just

to provide information so that they will do what we think is best, but to show them *how to choose between the right and wrong* information. This distinction will be the dividing line between those with generic morals who choose the wrong path by good intentions, and those who by discernment choose the right path. Providing our kids with life principles is one of the most effective ways that we can do this.

Say for example, one morning over breakfast, your daughter comes to you with a dilemma. She is going on a field trip and was wondering if she should bring a jacket. The answer is yes, see you later! If this were a math problem on a test, we as parents would never just give the numerical answer, but instead, show the child how to arrive at that answer. A practical or relational issue is no different!

Rather than give her the answer that you have already worked out in your head, walk her down the pathway on how to arrive at this conclusion. Allow her to consider different options while guiding her down the road to the best answer, and, depending on the size of the possible negative consequence, allow her to make the decision. This is an opportunity for her to learn by both your words as well as the outcome of her choices. Bringing up a story in the Bible to help her relate to another's experience will also assist in teaching her wisdom on how to rightly divide and personally apply God's Word.

You could mention the time David was about to fight Goliath. King Saul offered David his armor, which the young shepherd tried on but found too bulky to fight in. David then chose to use his own sling, which he was more comfortable with, and then went down to the stream bed to choose some rocks to bring along. Now, why would he choose more than one rock? Wasn't there only one giant? David knew the principle that *it is better to have it and not need it, than to need it and not have it!* Could he have also brought along Saul's armor just in case, then? Probably not, since it was so heavy, so he had a decision to make: what was the middle ground between bringing too much and too little? If David brought too little, what would have happened if he then missed with that first stone?

In the same way, let your daughter know that she has a choice to make. She has the choice to take a big bulky jacket, a lighter jacket, a fleece with layers, etc… Allow her to see her options, compare her choices to someone who has made wise decisions in the past, and come to her own conclusion. This takes much more time than simply giving the '*one size fits all*' answer, but will result in seeds of wisdom and discernment planted in your child which will bear fruit for the rest of their life.

DELAYED GRATIFICATION

Children are so full of wonder and quick to such contagious joy that we often long to see them experience it. It is critical to recognize, however, that although our desire as parents to see our children happy can be noble, without careful intention, it can also be destructive. We must stop and consider what principle the child is being taught when we do things to bring them joy. When we give in to the child's natural desire to have something new and cool, we are inadvertently teaching him a lesson in that moment about *how they are to deal with their own desires.* These are lessons that the child, as they grow into adulthood, will remember and apply when taking control of *(or submitting to)* their impulses and cravings.

1 John 2:16-17 teaches us about the lust of the eye and how it will never last! It has been

said that *it is easier to deny a desire than to fulfill those that follow*, so we must ask the question; are we teaching the child to master those desires or to give in to them?

There is an old axiom that warns us to "*govern your desires or they will govern you.*" Are we teaching our children how to decide what is truly worth spending money on, or just how good it feels to get that new toy, to show it off to friends, and then when that feeling wears off to chase after a new one? It's not hard to see how that pattern of thinking will manifest as an adult. The Lord gives us these moments as special preparation times so that the child can begin learning *the lesson of delayed gratification.*

The day after I turned twenty, I purchased a one-way ticket to Tucson, Arizona, caught a ride with a friend across the border into Mexico, and embarked on a journey that would last for as long and as far as my eighteen hundred dollars would take me. The duration of trip ended up reaching out to about three months, my money stretching that far due to hitch hiking, sleeping in hammocks, and meeting kind and generous people along the way.

About three weeks into the trip, however, I hadn't yet met anyone interested in hanging out with a dirty traveler, and I was still making my way through the desert, desperate to see the Pacific and plunge into its cool waters. I had planned to arrive at the ocean the following week, a place around a hundred miles farther down the coast which the locals had told me boasted nice beaches still unadulterated by tourists. In my desperation to be done with the desert and finally experience the coastal shoreline however, I decided I couldn't wait that long.

I asked some of the locals about a closer place I saw on the map that seemed to have promise, but they all shook their heads and urged me not to waste my time, but to instead wait and go to the nicer beaches farther south. Undeterred by their dissuading comments and no longer able to control my unquenchable drive to jump in the ocean, I bought a ticket for the next bus heading to my X on the map. In my haste I had forgotten to exchange a traveler's check for local currency (*ATM's in that part of the country still being a thing of science fiction films*), but just figured I would cash one when I got to the beach town.

When we arrived, I was deflated to find that what I had hoped to be a beach was no more than a small, rocky fishing boat inlet that wreaked of rotting fish parts and was littered with the same. There was no possibility of swimming, even for a minimalist like myself. With no other options, I decided to grab the next ride back to the previous town, only to be told that the bus I came in on was the last one, which had already returned. I shook my head and decided to grab a hotel and catch the bus out of there in the morning. Once I finally located the one hotel in the entire fishing village, I promptly realized that I had no cash. Asking the hotel clerk if he could direct me to the closest bank, he pointed over my shoulder in the direction of the town I had just come from, thirty miles east. I pursed my lips and stared right through him.

After about an hour of pacing up and down the street punching walls, I finally calmed down enough to swear that I would never again choose the more expedient path over the best one. This promise to myself didn't really take, but the sentiment held. At that moment, a small flatbed truck ambled by, loaded down with people hitching a ride back to the very town I had just come from, and so I instantly threw my backpack on the bed and hoisted myself aboard. It so happened that I had a couple of loose coins in my pocket that seemed to be just the right amount to restrain the driver from kicking me off, so my self-induced problem was solved. As harmless as the situation turned out to be, that little lesson forever stuck in my mind; *there are better things out there if you're just able to wait.*

The principle of delayed gratification doesn't just apply to money and possessions, but those *are* two clear avenues to learn it. When Jesus encountered two siblings fighting over an inheritance, He gave them one of the most impactful teachings on possessions that we find in scripture. *"Watch out! Be on your guard against all kinds of greed; life does not consist in the abundance of possessions," (Luke 12:15).* This alludes to the idea that the world will be speaking a lie to our children, saying *"the more you have, the better life will be,"* and it will be up to them to combat that deception with the tools that we give them.

How stereotypical is it when we see movies of people who have reached the pinnacle of their area of expertise *(usually financial)* only to find themselves even emptier than when they began? We recognize this when watching films, but how often and easily do we fall into the same trap, or worse, lead our children to do so? Every time the choice is presented to add another possession to my child's inventory, we must ask the question, *"What lesson am I teaching them?"*

In John 15:16, Jesus reveals that the reason He personally chose us was so that we would *bear fruit*. In The Parable of the Sower, Jesus spoke about the weeds that grew and choked the seed and *kept it from producing fruit. "But the cares of the world, the deceitfulness of riches, and the desires for other things enter in and choke the Word and it proves unfruitful..." (Mark 4:19).* Therefore, we know that one of the main purposes God has called us to accomplish in this life is to *bear fruit*, and we see here how one of the weeds that will keep us from producing this fruit is *a desire for possessions*!

Is happiness found in a possession? Is fulfillment something that can be purchased? Are we giving our children a shortcut to fleeting and artificial joy by offering them what their flesh wants in the moment, or are we leading them down the path to true joy that is found in self-control, denial of the flesh, and the ability to tell themself *'no'*?

The child who desires and finds imitation joy by receiving new toy after new toy will become the adult who falls into the empty pursuit of seeking fulfillment in new acquisitions or simply falls to the endless pursuit of *the exhilaration of the new*! This deception puts a person on the path to be an adult child who will spend their time and money pursuing things which will ultimately choke out any hope of real fruit in their lives.

A toy should be a reward for a special event or accomplishment, not a fix for the next dopamine hit. Even if the child isn't just *given* the toys, but they are allowed to spend their own money on frivolous things, consider what patterns you are helping them set for the rest of their lives. Encourage the child to take time and consider if the item is something that they need and will use, or if it's just a momentary desire that will pass. This looks practically like allowing them to see the item a few times over a period of several days or even weeks while telling them they can't have it right now, and to keep thinking on it. If they still want it after the time has passed, then it can be considered. In general, the higher the price, the longer the wait, but the principle of stewarding God's resources well is consistent on items of low and high price alike. Luke 16:10 displays this truth when Jesus tells us that, *"One who is faithful in a very little is also faithful in much, and one who is dishonest in a very little is also dishonest in much."*

One of our jobs as parents is to teach our children how to manage what God has entrusted to them, not how to use it to please themselves. It is imperative to teach the truth that the money we have isn't really ours, rather it is something entrusted to us for a short period of time from the Father, and we will have to give an account to Him on what we did with it.

If the opportunity to teach this life lesson is missed, then the child will gravitate to the mishandling of resources, and to ultimately spending that which God has entrusted to them on frivolous and empty things. Moreover, (*and more seriously*) they run the risk of believing that the deep longing in their soul is meant to be filled with physical and finite items, rather than by the God who created and loves them.

For parents who have found themselves, or unintentionally led their children down a path of dopamine addiction through compulsive (*although possibly well intentioned*) buying, the path back is a longer one, but it all starts with embracing the word '*no.*' Lead them to walk in delayed gratification. We will know the child has matured in this area when we can deny their request and be met with a response of acceptance or at least indifference rather than a melt-down.

Remember, in the beginning, especially to the immature, *righteousness looks like bondage but ends in freedom, while sin looks like freedom but ends in bondage.* Let us be mothers and fathers who lead those who follow us down the path of righteousness and freedom by first living and then teaching self-control!

BE THANKFUL - AND RESILIENT!

    The first trick that Satan used on Adam and Eve was to present the lie that there was something better outside of the Lord's will, and God's rules were holding them back from it. This deception can be seen at every level and at any age - and can be very convincing.

    I am from Washington and my wife, Folake, is from Nigeria. As our daughters grew, they just assumed that moms were black, and dads were white. As they got older and met other kids' parents, they started to ask the question, "I*s it supposed to be this way?*" What if both parents were supposed to be black, or white? Do other kids have it better? The enemy was already trying to sow the lie that happiness is somewhere else, and that changing the unchangeable could somehow make life better. This prompted some good, healthy discussions in our family and an opportunity for our daughters to realize and be thankful for the incredible gift that a multicultural family truly is.

    Children don't know what's best for them,

so giving a child what they want whenever they want it, *especially when they whine*, will create (among other things) an adult who complains and makes others miserable when they don't get their way. This kind of person is not only unbearable to be around but opposes God's exhortation in Philippians 2:14-15 to *"do all things without grumbling or disputing, so that you may be blameless and innocent."*

In the book of Exodus Chapter Sixteen, the people of Israel complain and grumble against Moses and Aaron over food. Moses then confronts the Israelites about it, clarifying that *they are actually grumbling against God*, not him. We must realize that when we complain, we are in reality, complaining that God isn't good and hasn't given us what we need - which is a lie! This is a similar lie to the one spoken to Adam and Eve mentioned earlier, which ultimately led them into one of the costliest decisions of all time.

One simple way to walk a child towards the discipline of thankfulness is to encourage them to talk normal when they want to whine. This can be difficult at first, because as a baby, when things weren't right their natural response was to cry. To go from crying to whining is a good step but it is incomplete until the choice is made to change from whining to saying *"please"* in a normal tone.

This is a healthy way to show someone how to control themselves and act nicely when they are hungry or don't feel like it, and if this lesson can be learned and applied in a benign scenario like whining, it will then be an available tool for attitude control to use in more important future situations. Never reward whining. Encourage them to ask politely and to follow it up with "*thank you*." Although these seem to be just words, they are disciplines that lead away from a demanding, complaining spirit and into a heart of thankfulness.

A helpful tool to use in encouraging a heart attitude of gratefulness as the child grows is simple sign language. Signs for *please* and *thank you* can assist in non-verbal connection as they grow out of the use of crying as their main avenue of communication but have yet to develop the skill of speech.

Not long after I got my driver's license, I decided to take a trip with my cousin to my grandparents' house on the Puget Sound. It was early summer, and having just gotten out of school for the year, we were ready to cast off the shackles of civilized society and seek out adventure. After a couple days of swimming, hiking and taking the old rowboat out to fish with hand lines, we were ready for a more daring excursion.

As the day was nearing its end, one of us had the idea of seeing how far into the sea we could row, and being that there was only one way to find out, we jumped into the rowboat and set off. As the light commenced to wane and the shore grew smaller and smaller, the wind began to pick up.

We didn't notice it at first, being in the midst of an argument, but as the waves grew in response to the increasing gusts we started to get concerned. We continued our heated disagreement, however, and were just reaching a point where the only thing we agreed on was that we didn't want to be friends anymore. By this time, the shore was a respectable distance away, and so, being sufficiently done with our adventure together, I decided to turn the boat around.

By then the waves had increased to the point where some of them were beginning to splash over the bow of our little ten-foot craft, while the wind, whipping salty spray off of the white caps, soaked our t-shirts which now hung on hunched and shivering shoulders. Our attitudes turned from indignant to solemn as we realized the difficulty of getting to shore through the menacing waves compounded by the rapidly growing gale.

At that moment, while in the midst of a slightly panicked rowing frenzy, an echoing *crack* rang out as the left oar suddenly snapped in half. I gazed down at the handle still clutched in my quivering hand as the lower half disappeared into the waves. I looked up at the stricken face of my cousin as reality set in. He immediately lurched to the front of the boat and frantically began to paddle at the water with his cupped hands while I remained in the middle, desperately slapping at the waves with the last remaining oar as if in a canoe.

It's hard to gauge the passage of time when you're struggling for your life, but the entire duration of that trip was filled with successive volleys of prayers, shouts, and somber silences as we fought every inch of our way back to shore. When we finally got close enough to touch the bottom, we both jumped in and pulled our boat to land, literally falling on our knees and thanking God for saving us from a cold and watery grave.

Not long before, we had each been ready to throw the other one off of the boat, and yet here we found ourselves hugging each other, laughing, and thanking God together! When we saw how close we had come to losing what really mattered and recognized the previously unappreciated blessings that God had given us, our hearts changed.

Keeping our children in a constant state of comfort and supply is unhealthy. Take your kid out of their comfort zone and get them away from their security blankets. Bring them into situations that will challenge and remind them of the everyday blessings that they have overlooked and thus taken for granted.

The principle of fasting works on every level. Teach your kids to put aside some good things in their lives for periods of time in order that they may learn the gift of thankfulness. Go camping, do screenless weekends, teach them to exercise, and lead them through something difficult. The cure for grumbling and complaining is thankfulness!

PUT OTHERS FIRST

An incredibly important aspect of relationship is the continued choice to *protect one another.* An individual who cannot control their temper or manage their emotions is a relationally toxic person that will cause deep wounds in those around them. A child who speaks hurtfully to their siblings becomes an adult who will speak hurtfully to their spouse and loved ones. Teaching children how to have good close conflict is essential to a healthy relationship in any form.

How did Jesus act when his friends betrayed Him? When His enemies taunted and tortured Him? When His followers abandoned Him? Did He respond in anger, puking His emotions on them, desiring for them to feel the pain He felt? Absolutely not. 1 Peter 2:23 tells us that, *"When He was reviled, He did not revile in return; when He suffered, He did not threaten but continued entrusting Himself to Him who judges justly."* This is our example! Jesus showed us exactly how to respond in times of difficulty and hurt. His response to His enemies is this – *"Father, forgive them!"*

One of the most accessible channels through which our children can learn and practice loving others and putting them before themselves is their siblings. So often siblings waste their years in the same home together hating one another, only to finally realize the treasure that a sister or brother truly is once they have moved out and only have access to each other from a distance. This is such a wasted opportunity to have the most unique relationship and special bond with a person that truly is like no other.

The main reason that sibling friendships struggle is due to the lack of relational leadership on the parent's part. One simple way to foster love between siblings is to talk to each of them privately and tell them how much their brother or sister loves them. This truthful input plants seeds of reciprocal love in children and leads them to naturally position their hearts openly towards one other. Who doesn't look kindly on someone who loves them? Take time, notice and relay to your children good things that the other has said about them when they weren't around. This will breed trust and anticipation of a positive environment that both will look forward to sharing with one another.

The most common reason sibling relationships struggle is because parents allow them to be hurtful towards each other. Regardless of whether it is physical, emotional, or verbal, not one hurtful word or action towards a person's brother or sister should *ever be tolerated* by a parent. If and when a hurtful action is taken from one sibling to another it must be handled with the utmost level of seriousness. Everything stops. The entire family machine grinds to a halt until this is dealt with. When we value the relationship that our children have with each other enough to prioritize it above our own time, convenience, hobbies, and personal lives – *so will they.*

When my sister, Rachel, was around ten years old our mom had to leave for the day and decided to put her in charge of me. I was six at the time, and before my mom headed out, Rachel had some questions she needed clarified, most importantly, whether or not she could spank me.

Our mother was very good at prioritizing our relationship, and so all of our lives Rachel and I have had a very close, healthy friendship. However, not long before this day my sister and I had hit a bit of a rough patch. Earlier in the week we had been tasked with cleaning out the barn before my parents got home, and since we hadn't finished it, our parents had given us an ultimatum; if the chore wasn't accomplished the following day before they got home, there would be consequences.

The next day we found ourselves in the barn, loading wheelbarrows full of muck to take out and dump in the manure pile. As luck would have it (*Rachel's luck, that is*), she became a little too bossy for my taste, and I decided I didn't want to clean out the barn anymore. In spite of her screeches, I sat down and began to ponder the questions of a six-year-old mind, like what bark on trees is made out of, and why are the worms in manure all white and sickly looking, when the ones in the dirt are all fat and healthy? After some time putting up with Rachel's incessant demands, I finally went to the door of the barn and began to shovel the manure *back* inside. She had to learn.

Suffice it to say, we didn't make the cut off time for the barn cleaning, and since Rachel was the oldest and most responsible (*Dad's words, not mine*), she carried the burden of those consequences. This brings us to the moment that mom was leaving the house and Rachel was asking for corporal punishment rights.

"If I'm responsible for him," she reasoned, "then I have to have the authority to motivate him, right?" She made a strong point, and I watched with dread as mom was convinced to grant Rachel legal spanking rights over me.

The reasons behind the next ten hours of

spanking that I received have been the subject of years of debate between my sister and I, but let's just leave it with this; I never again sabotaged her barn cleaning.

As radical as that story is, Rachel and I have had a great friendship all throughout our childhood, which still continues to this day. We attribute this to our mother's strict adherence (*except for that one time*) of prioritizing our relationship, and always (*except for that one time*) leading us to treat each other with love and deference, esteeming one another higher (*except for that one time*) than ourselves. We must likewise lead our children to be kind and loving to one another!

Tommy Nelson tells a story of an elderly woman in his church who stood by her husband's grave as they were laying him to rest, put her hand on the casket and said, "Seventy years together and he never once hurt me." Can you imagine living with someone like this? Someone who speaks with tenderness, intentionality and love? Someone who takes control of themselves in times of difficulty and hurt, who doesn't spew out frustration in the heat of the moment, but responds with patience and kindness? This all starts in childhood! Proverbs 12:18, *"The words of the reckless pierce like a sword, but the tongue of the wise brings healing."*

EMOTIONAL CONTROL

Allowing children to throw tantrums with no consequence creates adults who throw fits and expect good results to come from them. They become people who will act unreasonably in times of frustration and will blame others for the fallout. This produces an adult who is a grown child who is the center of their own universe; someone who, in times of heightened emotion, elevates themselves *(intentionally or not)* to the position of the most important person in the room. No one enjoys being with someone who acts this way, and this lack of control translates into all areas of a person's life, including and most detrimentally, their relationships.

Someone who lives with a tantrum thrower will have the unsavory choice of either being in constant conflict when things don't go the other person's way or going underground to walk on eggshells until it blows over. Don't raise your child to be like this! Parents who sit quietly by and allow their children to scream and cry and throw fits while the whole room suffers must realize that they are teaching this child that, as an adult, they have the right to disrupt the lives of those around them until they get what they want.

Teach them the lesson that when things don't go their way, it's not someone else's problem, and their disappointments don't give them the right to disrupt the lives of others. There are worse problems to endure than things not going one's way, and the consequences you choose for the child's tantrum should reflect that.

In the area of Emergency Communications, call takers are trained in a very simple technique called "*calm, simple, repetition,*" mixed with "*rewording the message.*" This happens exactly how it sounds. When someone has lost control of themselves and is in extreme emotional distress, one way to back them off of the ledge is to calmy repeat a clear, simple phrase, changing it slightly here and there until they come back to reality.

When I worked as a call-taker/dispatcher for a 911 facility, these kinds of emotionally distressed calls were common place. One evening when I picked up an emergency call, all I could hear on the other line was someone screaming over and over again, "Help! Help! Help!" Our conversation went something like this. (*When reading this, narrate my voice in the same voice you would use as you are putting your elderly grandmother to bed.)*

"911, what's the address of the emergency?"
"Help!"
"Ma'am where are you at?"
"Heeeelp!"
"Ma'am, I need to know where…you…are."
"Heeeelp!"
"Ma'am I'm going to send help, but you need to tell me where you are at.
"Just get heeere!!!"
"Ma'am, I need you to get ahold of yourself so I can help you, what city are you in?"

There was a slight pause, and I could almost hear the woman blink a few times as she suddenly stopped and realized her screaming wasn't changing the situation. After some more prompting, she angrily told me she was on the highway. As our conversation inched along, I was able to discover which highway she was on, an approximate mile post, and what the emergency was that she was dealing with. Her emergency, as it turned out, was that she was driving on the highway in a heavy downpour of rain and somehow one of her windshield wipers had slipped off, making it extremely difficult for her to see, and causing an unacceptable delay in her schedule as she pulled off to the side of the road and waited. She was then transferred to the State Patrol operator.

Emotional meltdowns are not rational. This

holds true for both children as well as adults, but the only way we can lead someone back into control of themselves is if *we ourselves remain calm and in control.* In our book, *"Close Conflict,"* the idea of emotional vomit is touched on, which is the process of allowing one's emotions to build up and then to explode all over the closest recipient, expecting them to make sense of it all. The Father has called us to have self-discipline, to take hold of our emotions, and to sort through them in order to distinguish what is happening in the situation before speaking.

It is not someone else's responsibility to sift through my frustration, rage or anger in order to determine what is going on in my heart. The responsibility is mine alone. The main way that we as parents teach our children to control their emotions *is by example.* Do I as a parent dump my annoyances on my child when they are loud, and I'm irritated? Do I lash out in frustration when my kid spills on the carpet right before we are walking out the door? When I'm late and I can't find my keys and it then turns out they were in my kid's pocket the whole time, is my reaction soaked in kindness and restraint, or thinly veiled irritation? Am I giving them an example of how to let someone know that they disappointed me, or *how to contain myself and walk through difficult situations with love and patience?*

Children aren't equipped to handle an

adult's emotions, and when we as parents raise the emotional level in the room, our children will follow suit. Conversely, as the emotional intensity rises with the situation, but we approach it with a calm voice and a patient heart, the atmosphere in the room will not only be calmed, but the child will also now see your actions and soon follow your example.

Our children will rise to the level of expectation that we place on them. This is why we see videos of five-year-old children in third world countries cooking meals for their younger siblings, carrying and comforting their infant sisters and brothers, or working skillfully at a difficult task for their parents' business. I don't say this to encourage taking away a kid's childhood in order to work, but to illustrate the fact that children will rise and adapt to whatever reality they are presented with.

Picture a mother and her friends sitting around the living room, spending time together while her child runs circles around the house. As the child rounds the corner, his foot slips and he face plants right in front of the crowd. A gasp erupts from the group, and they begin anxiously asking him if he is alright. The child just had a rather unpleasant experience and has been instantly filled with emotions of pain, fear, and embarrassment, among others. He doesn't know what to do with these emotions, so rather than standing up, brushing himself off and making a wry comment to ease the tension, he bursts into tears.

When given a choice on whether to melt down or rise in self-control, a child will usually choose the former unless he is led otherwise. If the accident results in obvious or serious injury then it is a different story, but for ninety-nine percent of situations you should never ask the child if he is ok; *tell him he is ok*. Speaking life and identity to the child in difficult moments will plant seeds of truth in their hearts which will echo back to them in future times of trial and hardship. *"You're alright, you're tough! Wow, I'm impressed, you are so resilient! You got this, get up and try again!"* Even if your heart is aching for their skinned knee, don't allow your emotions to convince them that they are fragile, rather encourage them that they are tough and resilient. As in all intense situations, be careful not to make the child deal with your emotions on top of their own.

Tenderness, recognition of a tough break, and comforting the child is by no means disregarded in these moments, but *the goal is to continuously lead them to be a person who isn't sidelined by pain*. An important part of our mission as parents is to raise a leader who is able to comfort others in the midst of their own hardship. Galatians 6:2 tells us to, "*bear one another's burdens,*" not make others bear your own!

DISCIPLINE OUT OF LOVE

Proverbs 23:14 – *"Discipline a child and save his soul from Hell."* All can agree that this is a pretty foundational goal for any parent. Discipline is essential, but it must be done right. There has been a pushback movement against physical discipline in America since the 1960's, but lately this resistance has been championed by people who have been abused or physically disciplined wrongly by someone out of frustration, anger, or sin.

Physical discipline from a place of frustration or anger is always wrong. God disciplines the children He loves and approves of, but He never disciplines them out of frustration. Discipline, both physical and otherwise, must only be done from a place of love and patience. A child must know what the rules are as well as what the consequences are, and both must be walked out in a calm and loving way.

One evening, when I was around the age of six, I had one of many interactions with my mother that resulted in the highest and most dreaded level of punishment: *spanking.* As she usually did, my mom calmly told me the verdict and the upcoming sentence before sending me to my room to await the consequence. My actions in this season had been leading to a plethora of spankings and frankly, I was getting tired of it. Since changing my actions or attitude didn't seem like a viable option at the time, I decided to try another way.

When mom entered the room holding the spanking spoon, I dutifully put my hands on the wall and awaited the incoming discipline. As she drew back and let go with the first blow, she was surprised that, instead of the usual *smack* of the impact, she heard a cold and resounding *crack*. Mom quickly realized what had happened and, before she could even demand that I remove the book from my pants, burst out laughing. She laughed so hard that she couldn't even continue dishing out my punishment, and the spanking was over. My plan had worked! Humor had saved me from discipline, and I was off the hook. It was a short-lived victory, however, as I soon found out that my dad didn't have the same sense of humor and finished the job.

My mom was so good at disciplining out of love. All of my life she excelled at being very tough but extremely fair. Kids can always tell when a parent is training them out of love or reacting to them out of anger and frustration. One leads to a lesson, while the other leads to contempt.

Public shaming and ridiculing only produces guilt and hiding, and like we see in Second Corinthians, *worldly sorrow leads to death*, not repentance. There are times when the discipline must be immediate without an explanation up front, but for the most part discipline, even spanking, must but done in a meek and humble way. Sit down with the child, look them in the eye and speak to them clearly. Explain how they knew the rule, they broke the rule, and now they are getting the consequence for their actions.

This is not a time for the child to bargain, argue, excuse or explain. *Clarifying and being sure that you're not punishing an innocent person is important*, but once you are sure the crime has been committed and a rebellion has occurred, then the child's only response should be a clear acknowledgment when you ask them if they understand. This is the time for them to listen to you and wait for the consequence, which can be just as agonizing as the actual consequence!

An extremely important component to

discipline is the breaking point. Our goal is never to crush the child's spirit, but instead to break their will. Disciplining out of the flesh always leads to a wounding of the child's spirit, while disciplining out of love leads to a breaking of their will. As Jesus was approaching the greatest victory in the history of mankind, the prayer that He spoke to the Father was this; *not my will, but yours*. Our goal is to align ourselves, our rules and our lives with the Father so that when we discipline our child, their own will is broken and then replaced with the will of the Father. This is why we must never discipline a child for annoying us or for merely having caused a problem, but rather for *the heart position of choosing the wrong path.*

You know your child well enough to be able to distinguish where the breaking point is, but in general it comes with tears. If you spank them with a gloved hand on their snow pants, then you most likely aren't going to break their will. If they are still angry and shouting at you after you've disciplined them then their will has definitely not been broken.

Bring them to their breaking point and then draw them back in close with love and intimacy. Job 5:18 speaks of the Father's discipline when it says, *"He wounds but he also binds up; He injures but His hands also heal."* Discipline is an aspect of God's love, and it is a seamless but critical transition to step from the harsh world of discipline into the loving place of tender reconciliation.

When we discipline out of love, we teach our children that the Father disciplines out of love, and when they make a mistake, the first and best thing they must do is to run back into His arms. The goal is to show them how He is trustworthy in His discipline and when we receive it with a good heart He will always lead us back into loving restoration.

"The wrath of man does not produce the righteousness of God." – James 1:20

CONSEQUENCES

One of the most important keys to being a parent is paying attention. Misrepresenting God by being distracted from relational connection with the child gives them the impression that the true Father doesn't take careful notice of every aspect of our lives. God is never distracted from us. He doesn't sleep and he is never away on vacation when we need Him.

Don't be the parent that mutters idle threats which aren't followed through with, makes promises that won't be kept, or stares at your phone as your child tugs on your sleeve and screams until you finally shake out of the stupor and notice them. *Pay attention and be mentally and emotionally available.*

If you tell your kid to do or not to do something, *you are on the hook to make sure it is followed through with.* One of the most effective ways to help a child develop the skill of self-motivation is, once you've given a directive, to pretend like you're not paying attention while still observing them like a hawk. Watch them out of the corner of your eye and be ready to reward or discipline accordingly. This helps lead the child to develop the habit of following through with something whether they think you are looking or not, which translates into an adult who has integrity before the Lord.

A child who learns that they can negotiate the consequences for their actions becomes an adult who believes they can live how they want to and negotiate the consequences with God later on. One important principle to implement beforehand is *"The principle of the republic."* A republic is a system built on laws and corresponding consequences that are created and communicated beforehand, allowing those living in the society to be aware of them in advance. These are not laws that a ruler arbitrarily implements in the moment depending on their current mood or relationship with a favored citizen or despised peasant. All are under the same rules and their predefined consequences.

As a child, were you ever in someone else's house and got in trouble for breaking a rule that you didn't know existed? Even as a child the injustice of this is obvious, so how can we as adults give the impression that God is like that? Never punish a child for breaking a rule that they had no clue existed, rather be diligent to communicate to them clear rules and their relative consequences. Consequences are set in motion the moment that the choice has been made, the rule has been broken, and the jury has just come back with the guilty verdict. At this point there's no longer an option to change one's actions; *only to have courage to face the judge.*

When I was around the age of seven my family went to visit my grandparents on my mother's side. They lived right near the beach on Whidbey Island in an amazing log house that just happened to be down the hill from my second cousin's place, who was about the same age as I was. One afternoon as we were looking for something to do, my cousin suggested we chase their chickens.

"Are you allowed to do that?" I asked doubtfully.

"For sure," he responded. "I do it all the time."

I studied his face, searching for any sign of guile that would indicate one of his usual tricks.

"I don't know," I said after a moment. "We're not supposed to do that at my house."

Normally I would have jumped at a chance to enter a chaotic adventure, but after having received some serious spankings a couple years earlier for that exact offense, I was cautious.

"I guarantee it," my cousin assured me. "My

mom says I can do it any time I want."

Somewhere in the depths of my memories I recalled hearing how laws in other countries were different from ours here in the states. As I mulled this thought over, I reasoned that since this place was so close to Canada maybe things were just done a little differently here...? Having already tasted the thrill of chicken chasing years ago (*before having it soured by my dad's belt*), something in me craved to feel that rush of the pursuit once again and so, shaking off my concerns, I decided to take advantage of the lax laws in this foreign land.

About three minutes into our chicken chasing mayhem, I looked up to see my grandfather standing at the coop entrance with a belt in his hand and a grim look on his face. I slowly turned, stone-faced, to my cousin who stood there shrugging with a sheepish grin. My entreaties for mercy due to ignorance fell on deaf ears, and I once again reaped the end of all who go after ill-gotten gain.

I will never forget how betrayed I felt, not by my cousin (*who didn't even get spanked*) but by my grandfather. In my heart, I truly was innocent of wrongdoing, and being punished for breaking a rule that I didn't know existed did not come across to me as discipline, but rather injustice. Towards the end of his life, I was able to share this story with my grandfather from my perspective, over which we both had a good laugh, and he assured me he was sorry for the mistake.

Little seven-year-old me eventually recovered from that mishap, but I have always remembered the bitterness of being punished for breaking a rule that I didn't know about, and have considered that lesson every time that I had to discipline one of my children.

One of the most important truths we can teach our kids early is that *God makes the rules, and we are subject to them.* We as people have no say in what is good or evil, but we have a simple choice between which of the outcomes we will reap; those from living what's right or those from living what's wrong. The key lesson that we must strive to impart is that no matter what, we can rely on the fact that the Father is trustworthy in all His judgements.

It is imperative to clearly communicate what the rules are, because *the punishment is not for the crime, rather it is for the heart that chose disobedience.* When the time for consequences comes, it is often a moment where the child wants to erase what they have done from memory, travel back in time, and choose the path that led to a better outcome. Whether this is from a repentant heart or a desire to avoid consequences no longer matters at this point. What is most important is communicating that our actions have consequences, *specifically the heart choice to do what they know shouldn't have been done.* The lesson here is that wrong choices can't be taken back and will be held to our account.

This speaks directly to the truth of God's Word where it tells us *"each of us will give an account of himself to God"* (Romans 10:12), *"and on the day of judgement people will give an account for every careless word they speak,"* (Mathew 12:36). Arguing, justifying and begging for the consequence to go away or be reduced are the cliché things that we see immature adults doing with the police as they are stuffed into the back of the patrol car.

Eliminating or reducing the consequence can be one of the most destructive things we do as a parent in these moments. The consequence they receive will be a direct measurement that they will use next time on whether or not what they did was worth the price paid, *especially when they are confronted with the temptation of doing it again.* When we allow a child to run away from us in order to avoid the consequences, or don't follow through with them upon the child's return, it teaches them that if they fall into sin as an adult, they can run away or avoid God long enough and the consequences will eventually dissipate. Never lose a race with your child in this situation! There are few more destructive things we can do to our child's character than to teach them that consequences to their actions might change if they argue, fight, or run away.

At the beginning of time, the Father made rules for Adam and Eve, and when the rules were broken, as painful as the consequences were, He followed through with them. When we as parents set consequences for our children's actions, it is imperative that we stand by them. When the consequences and discipline don't happen immediately, the child becomes an adult who sees God as someone who shrugs at disobedience and forgets about His Word, which eventually leads to a lifestyle of hiding sin, living in unrepentance, and believing the lie that nothing bad will come of it.

Psalm 119:75 *"I know, oh Lord, that your judgments are righteous, and that in faithfulness you have afflicted me."*

PRIORITIZE TRUE BEAUTY

Everyone wants to be desirable and attractive to different extents. This will manifest differently in females and males, but the longing to be approved and wanted is universal. So where does this desire go from being healthy to unhealthy? Jesus outlined the principle when he stated in Mathew 23:26, *"First wash the inside of the cup, then the outside will be clean."* Always start on the inside, then we can see clearly how the outside should look.

In the Song of Solomon, we see a picture of a teenager who is *(unknowingly)* about to meet her future husband. It gives an amazing look at where she is in life and what has led her to this point. Chapter One begins in the present day and opens with an older woman looking back on her life with her beloved. The scene unfolds as she recalls the years past, starting in verse five and opening with her as a young teenager working in a vineyard. Here we learn that her brothers were the ones who made her get a job, and because of this, not only has the sun darkened her skin, but she has not been able to take time to beautify herself like the other girls.

An important distinction to make in this scenario is that this isn't just a picture of a teenager working at a burger joint on the weekends to make some party money. Rather, with their father out of the picture, this job is an integral piece that she is playing to support her family. Her mother and brothers are depending on her, not to bear the entire financial burden, but bring in her share of their family's provision.

In those days (*as is still common*) a woman's skin was of great value, and taking care of it was a high priority for the sake of beauty and desirability. We see that, because of the authority that her brothers' have in her life, she is unable to devote time and energy to her looks.

Like most young people, she is dealing with insecurities surrounding her body and looks, and at the very least we see that she takes a wrong or low viewpoint of them. For some unknown reason her father is not in the picture, and we therefore see that her brothers have assumed the role of that authority in her life. It is interesting how the Lord uses a picture of a broken family to highlight a child raised right, illustrating that no matter the situation you find yourself in, you have the ability to put your family lineage on the right path!

It is by the brothers' directive that she has been spending her time working in the vineyard rather than devoting time to her looks, social activities, or attracting the opposite sex. Her responsibility to her family has superseded her desired devotion to her own outward appearance. In Chapter One Verse Six we see that the young woman assumes that her brothers are angry with her, and she believes that it is because of their anger that they have caused her to work and earn money for the family, rather than spend her time as she pleases.

How common is that? This is a clear depiction of the reality we see in almost every kid's life, where discipline and tough choices are misinterpreted by the child as the parent acting overbearing or unreasonable. How often, when faced with this response from a child, do parents, rather than calling the child to a higher standard, just avoid the conflict and allow their son or daughter to assimilate to the culture around them?

How many parents draw back from calling their child to a higher standard out of fear of losing the role of being their kid's buddy, or giving their child the impression that they're not the fun parent? Here's the even more important question; what was more beneficial to this girl, to have been allowed to use her teen years chasing her own fickle desires, or to invest those years learning to work hard, to submit to Godly authority, and to serve a purpose greater than herself? Which of these paths will create an adjusted person who can navigate the realities of life and adulthood?

As we find at the end of the Song of Solomon, it is a direct result of her submission to the guidance of the Godly authority (*in this case her brothers*) that she is brought precisely into the will of God and placed in the exact spiritual and physical location that will bring about her meeting the man that God prepared for her! This leads us to one of the most basic and yet crucial principles that we must recognize in order to trust the Lord in relationships; Satan will always offer us a shortcut to the reward which God has spent our lifetime preparing us for. If we take the shortcut it will lead to shipwreck and to the loss of what the Father desires to give us, but if we take the path Jesus is calling us to, while seemingly having more work and less play, it will lead to an even greater reward than we ever could have imagined! Sin always looks like freedom in the beginning, but ends in bondage, while righteousness always appears to be bondage at first, but ends in true freedom.

In Verse Five, we see how, although the

young teenager isn't very pleased with how she looks, a hidden part of her personality begins to emerge; *she likes who she is*. She says, *"I am dark but lovely."* Guiding a child away from the path of seeking or glorifying outward beauty and onto the path of prioritizing character will always result in recognition of self-worth. She still doesn't appreciate why her brothers have made her steer away from seeking her own will in order to work in the vineyard, but she is already experiencing the fruit of it!

Even the most outwardly beautiful people on the planet have things about their looks they dislike, and if they have been led to believe that the outward appearance is who they are, then they will inevitably dislike themselves. On the other hand, when a child is raised to understand the truth Peter defined in his epistle, which speaks of inward beauty, it will create a foundation of identity that they can begin to build upon; *"Your beauty should not come from outward adornment, such as elaborate hairstyles and the wearing of gold jewelry or fine clothes, rather it should be that of your inner self, the unfading beauty of a gentle and quiet spirit, which is of great worth in God's sight,"* 1 Peter 1:3.

When I turned sixteen years old, I had already saved up just enough money to purchase my first car, a 1981 Toyota Tercel. It didn't take me very long to destroy both the Tercel as well as my second car, learning the hard way that you're supposed to put oil in the engines if you want to keep them running. But once this lesson was securely planted in my brain, I set out in search of the third vehicle of my sixteenth year of life. When I saw the 1986 Suzuki Samurai, I knew it was the one. It had the look of a jeep, possessed four-wheel drive capability, and even had a convertible rag top that I could take off in the summer. On top of that it was cheap. Everything looked perfect to me about this car...from the outside.

As I drove my new purchase away from the seller *(who, to this day, is probably still rubbing his hands together)* my love for the car quickly began to fade. This was the most gutless vehicle I had ever or would ever drive. It had a top speed of around forty-five miles per hour on flat ground, and I don't even want to talk about what going up a hill looked like. Needless to say, I learned how quickly the charms of aesthetics wear off when presented with what is truly beneath the hood. That little car probably did save me from a pile of teenage speeding tickets, but it was little consolation to a heart betrayed by superficial beauty.

Proverbs 11:22 tells us *"Like a gold ring in a pig's snout is a beautiful woman who lacks discretion."*

How much easier is it to slap a new coat

of paint on a rusty car than to do all the hard work of dismantling, sanding and painting it well, or maintaining and overhauling the engine? No matter how much makeup, expensive clothing and jewelry is applied, it will never outweigh the true beauty of character. Outward attractiveness never makes up for the burden that a self-centered individual causes those around them to bear. There is nothing wrong with beauty, dressing nice and looking good, but like Peter reminds us, don't let that be the most beautiful thing about you! Let those things be an afterthought, adorning the already beautiful spirit.

TEACH GODLY AUTHORITY

In any relationship, whether business, social, or intimate, there must be a measurement of truth; a basis of right and wrong by which the parties involved can make unbiased decisions. God's word is the absolute standard on which we base every aspect of our lives and relationships. All of our own wants, desires, and opinions bow to the Word of God. When a child is allowed to treat a parent with disrespect, they begin to believe the lie that their feelings supersede what God says. A child who treats their parent with contempt will become an adult that treats the Heavenly Father as an equal who is subject to their own rationale.

The delusion of believing that one's own opinions override the truth of an Almighty God seems preposterous on the surface, but this is the mentality that the majority of the world lives with. A child who argues and talks back to their parent creates a grown person who must have their own way, regardless of whether they are right or wrong. Who wants to live with someone who will continue arguing to win a fight even if they're wrong? Defiance includes eye rolling, arguing, storming off or slamming the door, and refusing to obey a direct request. All of these, in any relationship, friendship, marriage or otherwise, are toxic actions that damage trust, wound hearts, and must never be allowed in a family.

Teaching someone else to submit to Godly authority is only possible, however, if we ourselves are submitted to His authority. Are we as leaders submitted to the Lord? John tells us that, *"he who does not love his brother whom he has seen cannot love God whom he has not seen."* This same principle applies to God's authority. If we are unable to come under the authority that He has placed on earth through His people and through the leaders that He has placed in His church, how could we say that we are under the authority of the One we cannot see?

Jesus told Israel that they would not see Him again until they said, *"blessed is he who comes in the name of the Lord."* This speaks to the truth that we won't be able to see the Lord rightly until we receive Him *when He comes to us through other people*, regardless of how they look or the imperfections that they carry. Racism, cliques, and prejudices stem from joining with or rejecting people based on what is seen on the outside, rather than the treasure that is beneath the surface. We will never be free of this type of evil until we truly say, "*blessed is he who comes in the name of the Lord,*" and begin to see God, His authority, and His face in those that He brings to us, as well as those that He places us in authority under.

When I was four years old my mother took me to a pediatrician for a checkup. At the time I wasn't feeling very well, and from what I've been told, I sometimes had the tendency to be a little difficult in those moments.

The doctor hadn't had much interaction with children (*or so it seemed*) and was apparently being a little blunt in his dealings with me as a four-year-old. I remember resisting some of the procedures that the doctor was attempting on me, and him ultimately strong arming their way to completion. He was getting frustrated with me, but I guarantee that feeling was mutual, and when he left the room momentarily, my mother leaned over and encouraged me that it was almost over and to just hang in there.

When the man returned, he stood with his back towards me and spoke to my mom, relating the results from the tests that had come back.

"I bet you don't even know what those big words mean," I told the doctor, my tone full of contempt.

"And you'll never know what they mean!" He shouted back and stormed out of the room.

God puts people in places of authority in our lives, whether they deserved the position or not. Choosing to honor or dishonor them based on how we feel or on how we gauge their worthiness is not an option. That pediatrician was not necessarily cut out to work with children, but I needed the skills he had to offer, regardless of his temperament, maturity level, or interpersonal communication skills. God will put difficult people in positions of authority all throughout yours and your child's life, and your kid needs to know how to honor them whether they approve of the person or not.

Honor is something so important to God that He promises to honor anyone who honors Him! This is one of the most exciting promises that He gives us; the God of the universe would honor us! The only way we can teach our children the path to receive this incredible blessing from the Lord is by first walking in it ourselves.

Proverbs 3:5-6 *"Trust in the Lord with all of your heart and lean not on your own understanding. In all of your ways acknowledge Him and He will make your paths straight."*

NO IS A GOOD WORD

One summer, shortly after turning fourteen, a friend Ryan and I were sitting around trying to decide what to do with our afternoon.

"What if we drive up to the lake?" Ryan offered up.

"I don't know," I hesitated, slightly grimacing, "I kind of got in trouble last time I did that."

I was referring to the year before, when my cousin and I had driven up to that same lake to shoot squirrels, the trip being abruptly cut short when we were arrested by a fish and game warden, not only for driving at the age of thirteen, but also carrying pistols and hunting without licenses. The adventure didn't end there, however, as the warden then proceeded to confiscate of all our firearms and call our parents, the day finally culminating in the accidental discharge of my cousin's rifle which blew a hole through both a door and a wall in our house.

Ryan looked at me with a bored expression and threw the decision back in my lap. "What else are we gonna do?"

I was never a person who cared much for doing things by the letter of the law, but for some reason that day I just didn't have a good feeling about this plan. I couldn't quite articulate why I felt we shouldn't do it, but that particular afternoon something just nagged at me not to go.

Since I had no intelligible answer to Ryan's question, however, we piled into our family's flatbed truck and rumbled up the mountain towards the lake. It was hot, and since our pickup lacked even the most basic of niceties, by the time we finally rolled up to the water both of us were covered in sweat.

"Let's go swimming," Ryan announced as we stepped out of the truck. As much as I desired to hit that cool water, I also hated the idea of walking around in wet clothes the rest of the day.

"I don't really think so," I argued, "all I brought are my jeans." But Ryan was already walking towards the shoreline.

"Let's just ditch our clothes!" He shouted as he tossed his shirt aside.

"Yeah," I stalled, "but sometimes there are

families having picnics up here."

Ryan stopped and looked around. "Do you see any families, Ross?" Since we were clearly the only ones in the vicinity I had no argument against this logic, and so we both piled our clothes in the reeds and dove into the lake. It really was a perfect day, and after getting our fill of swimming, we crawled up onto the shore and stood their laughing, beating our chests, and doing our best impressions of Tarzan screams.

"Go ahead and put your clothes on boys," a voice boomed from behind us, "and then come over and let's have a talk." We looked at each other in horror, and then turned to find two sheriff deputies standing there with tired looks on their faces.

As much fun as it can be to just head into the unknown and live at the behest of our every whim, sometimes a simple *"no"* can save us from so much trouble.

A parent who is unable to say *"no"* to their child creates a child who lacks self-restraint, and ultimately is unable to tell themselves *"no"* as they get older. Worse, it leads to an adult who has difficulty hearing and receiving a *"no"* from God. It is so much easier to say to a child, *"Let's not play with that,"* or *"could we please not hit?"* or worst of all to just allow the child's negative actions to continue out of one's own unhealthy desire to avoid conflict.

These approaches can come from a well-intentioned desire to protect the child's feelings, but it ultimately ends in a person unprepared for real life. If the child isn't taught that the word *"no"* is a good thing, then they won't grasp the power that it has when used against evil or temptation in their own life.

The parent isn't the one playing with the item, nor is the parent the one who is screaming too loud, or hitting their sibling; *the child is*! Trying to alleviate the child's burden of guilt by taking some of it on yourself does no favors for your kid, it only lessens the impact of your words by diluting the truth and avoiding immediate conflict, usually out of the fear of stirring up the child's defiance. If saying *"no" does* stir up defiance, then refer back to the section speaking on disciplining out of love.

Do the ten commandments say, *"Let's not commit adultery,"* or *"Please don't murder?"* Absolutely not. The Lord is never afraid to tell us directly what to do and what not to do. This all still must be said and done in love and gentleness, but it must be done. It has been said that *"clarity is kindness,"* and in the case of our interaction with our children this couldn't be truer.

Exodus 20:3. The Ten Commandments-- *"Do not..."*

SELF-CONTROL

Self-control is one of the most crucial abilities which possessing or neglecting will play a part in our success or failure in every aspect of our time here on earth. Here is the best news; it's a free gift! Paul tells us in 2 Timothy 1:7 that, *"God has not given us a spirit of fear, but of power, love and self-control."* Galatians 5:22-23 shows us that self-control is a fruit of the Holy Spirit, *"the fruit of the Spirit is love, joy, peace, patience, kindness, goodness, faithfulness, gentleness and self-control."*

Have you seen *(or been)* a parent in a social situation where the child is acting out, and instead of correcting their behavior, the parent just changes the surroundings to eliminate the need for confrontation? This is a waste of a teaching moment. Our goal isn't to make sure there are no bad consequences, but rather to teach the child how to make good decisions.

When our first daughter Ruth was born, we lived in an apartment complex in a large city in Venezuela. Our home had only the basic amount of furniture necessary for a small family of three, and so rather than have shelves for things such as lamps or house plants, we just kept them all on the floor. One of the plants that we had on the floor just so happened, we were told, to be poisonous.

When Ruth was around nine months old, she began to take her first steps and was soon walking. This led to the day that she curiously approached the plant. I could have easily moved the plant somewhere that she couldn't reach it, but instead I just watched the situation unfold. As she reached for the plant, I knelt beside her and clearly told her not to touch it. She looked at me and then continued reaching for it. Once more I repeated myself. She then reached out and touched one of the leaves. As much as it broke my heart, I flicked her little hand, and, in full disclosure, we both burst into tears. I then picked her up and comforted her and just lavished her with love and affection. Not only did she never touch that plant again, but she forever remembered the meaning of the word "*no.*"

If I had just put the plant on the counter, it would have been more expedient for me and fixed the issue that morning pain free, but there would have always been the fear that she might someday find a way to climb up and grab one of those leaves. Instead, that day Ruth learned a series of lessons and developed her first level of self-control.

Imagine a parent has their child in a shopping cart in the checkout line. As they pull up to the cashier the child begins to grab at the candy on the shelf while the mother begins to grasp at the child's hands, pulling a Snickers bar out of one hand while the child is grabbing for a Twix with the other. A child who must be restrained by a parent becomes an adult who must be restrained by others. In extreme cases it becomes the police's job to restrain this adult, but in most instances the duty falls to their spouse, which the absolute *worst* job in the world for a spouse to have.

Our goal as parents is to raise a child to be a person who has self-control. When we allow a child to keep wiggling off our lap after they've been told to sit still, to continue to grab the candy in the isle after being told not to, or to persist in pulling on the parent's hand to leave after they've been asked to wait, we are creating a person who must be restrained.

Instead of holding the child who is trying to wiggle off of the parent's lap after being told to sit still, let them know that if they get down, they will be in trouble. Whatever consequence you choose, let them know what it is, and be prepared to dish it out. Then, rather than restraining them, allow them to make the choice. If they choose to remain on your lap like you asked, wait a reasonable amount of time and them reward them by letting them get down. Never make the mistake of forcing them sit there for an hour until they eventually decide that the punishment would be better than the torture of following your request!

If your child is pulling on your hand or

continuously interrupting your conversation and declaring it's time to leave, gently ask them not to interrupt and to wait patiently. If they do it again, remind them calmly that you told them to wait patiently, and that if you have to tell them once more then they will be in trouble, but be ready to follow through with those consequences immediately. Don't be the parent who then proceeds to talk for the next couple hours while your kid languishes in wait for you.

Isn't this how God teaches us? He is gentle, gives us direction and different chances, but also allows consequences in our lives when we don't listen or obey. Do not hide the toy that they're not allowed to play with, don't leave the store because they can't behave, and don't put the plant up higher that they've been told not to touch. Make it very clear what the rule is, and when it is broken, don't restrain their hands and don't change the environment; bring the consequences. This teaches them the reality of life as an adult. When we are grown, God gives clear rules and doesn't restrain us from our choices. He allows us to decide and then receive either the rewards of obedience through self-control or consequences of rebellion.

Psalm 32:9 - *"Do not be like the horse or the mule, without understanding, which must be curbed with a bit and a bridle, or it will not stay near you."*

FEED THEM
HEALTHY FOOD

Towards the end of my twenty first year, I made the decision to sell everything I owned and buy a plane ticket to Venezuela for a mere one hundred dollars. The attacks of 9/11 had recently occurred, dropping the prices for airline tickets to just inside of my price range, and so I jumped at my chance to ditch the shackles of my hometown and go see the world.

My goal in traveling was to go as far and as long as I could on as little money as possible, and to ultimately find a place to settle down and call home. The journey began at the top of South America, and after a two-week bout with dengue fever which led to the introduction to my (*as of yet unrealized*) future wife, I was carving my way south along the coastline.

It was on the third month of the trip when I landed in Cuzco, Peru, a beautiful mountain city full of incredible Incan architecture. Although I had sold everything I owned, I hadn't really owned very much which resulted in my funds being extremely meager. Compounding that with the fact that a couple days before I had just been pickpocketed and lost my passport with all of my cash along with my entire savings in traveler checks, I was barely scraping by.

Since I had come that far, I reasoned that I should just make the trip to Machu Pichu which was only another day's journey down the road. My sister had recently joined me on my trip and had agreed to lend me the money until I could get my passport and traveler checks replaced the next week in Lima, which lay at the end of a miserable thirty-two-hour bus ride (*as well as a future mugging...*). But at that point I had my sights set on experiencing some amazing, ancient Incan ruins.

For the past few days, I had been subsisting on a steady ration of sliced beef heart and potato wedges, skewered on sticks, and lovingly cooked on the side of the road by locals over some burning tires. Each of these hearty meals cost me a mere twenty-five cents, and so I loaded up enough little shish kabobs for a couple days rations as our small group of friends hitched a ride on a corn truck in the direction of that ancient mountaintop town.

By the next day I was starting to feel a touch off, and the following evening found me the sickest I have ever been in my entire life. Sometime that night I was awakened in our little hostel by extreme nausea accompanied by a feeling of impending doom, and after crawling my way through pitch blackness to the tiny bathroom, I proceeded to fill both the toilet and the adjacent shower simultaneously with the contents of all of those cheap meals. The fact that I was literally throwing the last of my money directly down the drain mattered little to me as I spent the next six hours praying that the end would come soon, in whatever form it was to take.

A grave lesson that I took with me from that moment forward was this; *cheap food will cost you…dearly.*

This section is not speaking to mothers who enjoy cooking and serving their families different elaborate, healthy meals. This is for parents that cater to their child's refusal to eat foods that they aren't familiar with or don't enjoy. All food is an acquired taste, so give them a taste for nutritious food early. The child is a part of the family, not a little prince or princess that the mother must cater to! Even if the provider doesn't mind serving extra catered meals, treating a child this way gives them an unhealthy view of themselves, and sets them on a path to expect the same treatment from others, and eventually their spouse.

Sugary snacks, boxed cereals, chicken nuggets, hot dogs, corn dogs, boxed macaroni and cheese, fast foods… All of these are extremely unhealthy treats and should only be eaten on rare, celebratory occasions. The alarming truth is that so often this garbage is given to children for their everyday meals! It is no wonder that American children rate among the most obese, disease ridden, and unhealthy children in the world.

The reason children choose to eat junk food over healthy food is because they are given the choice! Any time a child is given the choice between something healthy or unhealthy, bland or sweet, difficult or easy, they will take the most immediately rewarding option, which is always the worst one for them.

In the same way that there is no junior Holy Spirit, there is no junior nutrition. Children need God's Word, and they need real food! Don't cook separate meals for your child except on special occasions like birthdays and so forth. One of our jobs as parents is to teach our children to make the most difficult choice when they are presented with one, and we can help them learn to do this by creating good habits and patterns for them to walk in.

Mathew 7:13-14 - *"Enter through the narrow gate. For wide is the gate and broad is the road that leads to destruction, and many enter through it. But small is the gate and narrow is the way that leads to life, and only a few find it".* We must teach our children to take the less attractive way.

THE RICHES OF AN IMAGINATIVE MIND

When our daughters were still small, we had the incredible fortune of meeting a family who, not only had daughters close to the same age as ours, but also had similar values, goals, and dreams that we did. We quickly struck up a close friendship with these amazing people and commenced doing life with one another, raising our children together, and eventually serving the Lord with each other. As our daughters spent more time with one another, we began to notice entire worlds that they would create with each other through story and imagination. It struck me one day, as our friends arrived at our house, that after greeting each other, the very next words out of our kids' mouths would always be, "*Let's pretend that...*"

We all became closely acquainted with the *"Kellingame Universe"* which consisted of a place called Kokokio in which dwelled kangerhumans, miss walkaways, and a myriad of other imaginative lifeforms. They would spend hours in this world while every so often taking a periodic break to go outside and play their favorite game of their own invention, "Hunted." There was never a moment when you would walk into the room and find these creative young girls on phones, tablets or screens. Sure, they would watch the occasional movie together, but this only led to more imagination games that would morph into a whole other invented world.

By the time that they were allowed to have phones, their minds and imaginations were so well rounded that their phones just became another outlet for creativity, which were used to make movies, commercials, and *"news break"* clips, rather than watching mindless videos or playing useless games. The key is not to simply remove or disallow all technology from our children's lives, rather it is to raise them intentionally so that their brain is able to develop enough to use that tech for their benefit. *Screens make great servants but terrible masters.*

Screens, phones, tablets, computers, etc... have incredibly positive applications in so many ways when applied to learning, rewards, and skill building for the future. The powerful potential of technology found in screens, both positive and negative, can be compared almost directly to the power of opiates, which is what both heroin and the pain killer oxycodone are derived from. When used in the right application, opiates are essential for surgery, post-operation pain regulation, and emergency pain control, but when used incorrectly, opiates lead to destroyed lives, addictions, and the crisis we know throughout the world as the Opiate Epidemic. In the right hands and for the right purposes, different medicines are used for good, while in the wrong hands they are drugs that destroy countless lives.

During the formative years, when a child's curiosity drives them to question, understand and explore the world around them, they will begin to lean on the boundaries provided for them while their brains yearn to learn and grow. How are we aiding their growth in this extremely crucial time?

When the child begins to be fussy, have overactive energy levels, or become a distraction to what we are currently involved with, what is our response? Are we recognizing the unique opportunity to teach and engage with our child, or are we handing them our phone to play games, watch videos or otherwise get them off our backs?

A child needs to be encouraged to go outside, to grow, explore, tip over rocks and look for bugs, or just sit in the car and look out the window! In the book of Romans Chapter One we are shown how God's attributes are clearly seen all throughout His creation. Are we taking our kids into nature to see the attributes of God or are we allowing them to stay cooped up in the house playing video games and watching screens?

Boredom is not a bad feeling which must be plied with the salve of entertainment, it is a natural reminder that our minds and bodies are needing to be kickstarted into gear and connected to the world around us. Going outside and engaging the body and mind is more difficult and much less comfortable than sitting inside and vegging out (*for both the parent and the child*), but one of these choices will bring growth while the other will stunt it. Remember, children always default to the easiest choice, so it is up to us as parents to lead them into the most difficult ones.

It is imperative to recognize the addictive power screens have - especially in children. When we employ screens as babysitters at any age it is crucial to be cognitive of the fact that we are teaching our children a negative lesson which leads to bondage, and the lie is this: *moments of discontent must be medicated.* How many adults are enslaved by this deception? The lie that life and free time should be spent on entertainment and self-pleasure, which in turn, biologically shapes minds to be dependent on dopamine hits that come from constant entertainment.

Screens are the enemy of imagination and creativity in children.

When we give children long or unlimited access to screens, we are conditioning their souls to respond to discomfort by seeking distraction and self-medication, leading to a disadvantaged adult who is unable to withstand hardship. Romans 5:35 *"...suffering produces endurance, and endurance produces character, and character produces hope."* How many people today are without hope and lost in depression simply because they cannot stand some slight suffering? Lead your children to be resilient adventurers who use boredom as motivation to create!

DEAL WITH IT

As the summer of '88 was drawing to an end, I was mentally amping myself up for the rigors of my next year long sentence in school. The stint I had done in second grade had been rough, but I had made it through, experiencing only a few scraps with some bullies in the yard at recess. My main concern, however, as I eyed the approaching third grade year, was a particular bully who no longer even went to the same school as me. For the sake of anonymity and the grace of new beginnings, instead of using his real name, I will just refer to the bully in this story as Adolf.

Adolf was a ninth grader who took a certain sadistic glee in the sufferings of us elementary schoolers, especially when he had us all to himself on the school bus. He lived in the same area as we did and thus rode the same bus, subjecting anyone smaller than him to his unique and capricious form of malice.

My mom and dad had taken our family to his house to visit his parents the week before for a bible study, which resulted in an hour of torment before I finally made a mad dash out of his room and back to the safety of the public eye. He was able to cling to the cuff of my pants for a few feet, but my little eight-year-old legs just dragged him along as I churned my way out the door and on to freedom. Such was my will to survive bullies.

For the first couple of months of third grade, I was able to sidestep any real confrontations with Adolf, and most of our interactions were fairly benign. I began to notice, however, that each time I ducked his ridicule, or shrugged off his taunts, he would grow slightly bolder and more injurious.

Then came the day. As we all piled into the bus, Adolf headed towards his place in the back while my friends and I took our seats in the middle. The first part of the ride was uneventful, and I became lost in thought, mentally preparing for whatever the warden had in store for our class that day. Suddenly my hat was knocked to the floor. I felt another sting as Adolf once again smacked the back of my head with his schoolbook.

"Knock it off, Adolf," I said with a scowl and downcast eyes.

"What are you going to do little baby," he taunted, "are you going to cry?" I shook my head and stared at my backpack.

"Ooo the little baby is gonna cry, waahhh!" Adolf laughed. His eyes then widened, and his expression became serious as he drew his face closer to mine.

"Are you going to cry little baby?" He asked

once again, with pursed lips.

In that instant I made a split decision, and in a flash, I lashed out and punched Adolf right in the mouth. The world turned silent as the entire bus drew a collective gasp. I looked down at my fist, wondering what it had just gotten me into, and for the longest moment deeply regretted my choice. Adolf's face lost all expression, and I began to steel myself for the beating that was about to come. But rather than attack, the eyes of that menacing bully began, instead, to fill with tears. I stared in disbelief, as did all of the other occupants of the bus, as his entire face began to contort into a soundless sob.

"Ross," Adolf stuttered, his voice cracking, "just leave me alone." And with that he turned, retreated to the back of the bus. That ended the brutal reign of Adolf, who never again bothered anyone of us on that bus.

This story is not promoting the idea that all conflict is to be dealt with physically, but rather to highlight the fact that avoiding confrontation only causes the inevitable future conflict to grow larger and more extreme in its consequences. Hiding from relational issues will not make them go away, neither will merely distracting or deflecting attention off of them. Issues are only solved when we deal with them.

Imagine two children playing on a living

room floor. Your friend's child is playing with a toy truck, and you notice your child eyeing it. He walks over, takes hold of the truck and starts pulling it away from his friend. Right away you recognize a situation that is about to explode, and so in order to keep everything copacetic, you grab another toy truck and quickly distract your child with it and diffuse the potential battle.

This is a very common response, mostly because it is quick and effective in deescalating a conflict and avoiding a scene. In choosing to deal with the matter in this way, however, an incredible teaching opportunity is missed, and what's more, the conflict is only postponed until the next time your child again wants what another has.

One of the most important things to remember in parenting through these types of situations is this: *our goal is to recognize each conflict as a powerful teaching moment, not as something we should avoid.* So often, much of parenting, indeed much of our lives, is spent attempting to avoid conflict. While there is some wisdom in saving your *"no's"* for when you need them, the truth is that God never avoids conflict!

We must begin to grasp the truth that conflict, when dealt with rightly, is a greater opportunity for deeper growth, intimacy and relationship than almost any other path. When we realize and accept this, we will not only stop avoiding conflict and instead begin to see it for what it is: *a unique chance to learn and grow together.*

Instead of grabbing a second toy and trying to bargain your child away from the first one, this is a valuable moment to teach and explain to the child the value of respecting someone else's property. You can direct them to a different toy afterwards, but make sure the important lesson gets taught first. Taking another's toy is never ok. This includes clearly telling them that they can't do that, taking a firm stance, and risking a possible meltdown. Keep in mind, dealing with a child's meltdown is much easier than dealing with a teenager's, or a grown man's meltdown.

Every time a parent just distracts the child away from doing the wrong thing, they inadvertently set an appointment for themselves to do it again at a later date, but with greater consequences. Our goal with our children is to teach them to control themselves so someone else doesn't have to, both while they are young as well as when they become adults. A child who is distracted from an issue rather than trained through it becomes an adult who will also avoid dealing with problems or conflicts, and instead turn to distractions when these types of matters arise in life.

THE RICHES OF PURPOSE

In early 2002 I was living on the Northeastern coast of Columbia and working as a dive master at a scuba diving school in a tiny fishing village called Taganga. This small town was nestled in a little cove and surrounded by cliffs that dropped off straight down into the water. The climate was the perfect combination of tropical and dry, as it marked an area where desert and jungle merged together.

I use the term "worked" rather loosely, as my only responsibilities were to go diving with the different groups that came through and to make sure everyone stayed safe and had a good time. In return, I got a free place to stay and all the free day and night diving I could ever want. My life in this little inlet, depending on the mood, consisted of swimming, scuba diving, spear fishing, guitar playing, octopus hunting, sunbathing and swinging in hammocks. Being that our little dive shop was a destination point in popular travel books, the warm, sunny days were always filled with a continuous inflow of backpackers, travelers and new people to meet and spend time with.

As amazing as all of this truly was, I began to recognize a deep desire inside for more than just a life of ease. I had left home eight months prior and had been living that entire time seeking how to have the most fun at the least cost. This lifestyle, although initially enjoyable, had begun to grow empty and old, and I was tiring of living out of a backpack. I had become weary of the streams of new friendships that didn't last for more than a couple weeks, as people inevitably packed up, went home, or moved on to the next town. I desired to grow roots.

The more I pondered this feeling, the more I realized that what I truly longed for was purpose. A purpose higher than people, organizations, or projects. Something that, although it was far beyond those things, also encompassed, formed, and guided them. This deep-rooted desire was what finally began to turn my eyes to God. It was only six months later that I found myself married, with a child on the way, and serving a purpose infinitely greater than myself.

We are created to serve. The path to the

greatest fulfillment is not a life of ease and comfort, but a life laid down for others. One of the most astounding attributes of our Savior is that he didn't come to be served, but to serve! If the God of the universe, who has access to ministering angels to attend to His every need, came to serve His creation, how could we teach our children to do anything less?

Nature shows us how continuous comfort without struggle is unhealthy for any living thing, and therefore, reason tells us that difficulties and challenges are essential for growth and development. This is true physically, mentally, emotionally and spiritually. Have we stopped to consider the damage that we do to our children by providing them with the easiest, most comfortable lives possible? Kings all throughout history didn't live in the luxury that we have available to us today, but how has this effected our society? Have levels of depression, hopelessness, mental health disorders, and all-around contentedness increased or decreased?

Anyone who has visited impoverished nations can attest to the fact that people who only have access to a fraction of the affluence that we have in first world countries still somehow tend to express more joy and contentedness than we who have exponentially more. How can this be? The answer has many aspects to it, but a large part of it culminates in this: *persistent ease weakens the soul, while struggle strengthens it.*

Exercise is a principle that works both spiritually and physically, and unless we teach our children this truth, they will gravitate to the easiest choice available to them, inaction. The truism, *"a bustling mother makes a slothful daughter"* holds weight in every century, and ours is no exception. Many grow up without appreciation for their parents' hard work or servanthood, until they become a parent themselves and have to play catchup, not only learning the skills necessary, but also looking back on the time they lost while taking their parent for granted. Bringing your child alongside you in your chores breeds a child who can appreciate and walk in what it means to work and carry responsibility.

The added effort and time to teach someone a new ability often can tempt falling into the mentality of, *"if you want it done right you have to do it yourself,"* which is momentarily expedient, but ends up hindering a person who could otherwise gain a new life skill. We all know that doing a task such as folding laundry or washing dishes can be over and done with in just a few minutes when taken on by a skilled worker. However, to come alongside and teach someone with no experience the skills necessary to perform these tasks, although it takes twice as long and often incurs a mistake or two, will result in a myriad of benefits.

The point of teaching children how to do a skill isn't merely to lessen our workload, rather it is a way for them to find a piece of purpose in serving their family. Young people crave godly dignity just like adults do, whether they know it or not, and allowing them to use small portions of their life to serve their family or others is an amazing source of this. Teaching children to spend their life for something greater than their own gain is one of the most important mindsets that we can foster in them.

There is a leadership principle that advises us to *"only do what only you can do."* There are certain things that only a parent can do, such as working a career, paying bills, driving a car, etc., and then there are things that our children can do, or at least learn to do, such as cook, clean, do laundry, work on vehicles, maintain outside property, take care of animals…the list goes on and on.

Teaching them how to work is how we steward their future by not only training them in useful life skills, *but by giving them the opportunity to learn how to serve.* The extra time and energy spent on teaching a child is well worth the personal benefit they receive, not to mention the priceless sense of purpose that they gain from being a necessary and beneficial part of the family.

A mother who does their teenager's laundry,

cooks their food, washes their dishes and cleans their room will create a person who doesn't personally grasp the cost and value of serving. We must raise up people who are able and willing to parent others, not create people who must be parented by their future husband or wife.

Proverbs 22:6 *"Train up a child in the way he should go, and when he is old, he will not depart from it."*

PART 4

On the lookout

ON THE LOOKOUT

Our role as a parent is vast and comprehensive and includes countless joys and wonders that we get to experience and re-live with our children as they grow and interact with their environment for their first time. The innocence and light-heartedness of a child is contagious, and living in their world alongside them inevitably changes ours, and part of our job is to enter and enjoy this world of innocence. Notwithstanding, one of our highest priorities as a parent is the role of protector, and the safeguarding of their innocence is near the top of our duties to perform.

There is a principle stated by Jesus in Mathew 7:7, "...*Seek and you will find...*" One of the aspects that this speaks to is the idea that if we are on the lookout for something, we will find it. For example, if someone looks for something positive in a person or situation, they will usually find it. If they look for the negative, they will also find it. Our goal isn't to focus our eyes to look for negative signs, but rather to keep our eyes open to see the world around us rightly, or as the Lord told us in Matthew 10:16, our calling is to *"be as wise as serpents and as innocent as doves."* It is possible to remain in a place of innocence with our child while simultaneously recognizing the good and evil that is around us, all while using prudence to decide what should or shouldn't be allowed into their world.

The word "trauma" has been so overused and misused in our culture as to warrant the desire to avoid it, but the truth is that early traumatic events can deeply affect a child, and a kid's response to these events (*even subconscious*) can propel their life onto a completely unexpected and destructive trajectory. Early sexualization through another person or pornography is one of the most common and yet overlooked ways a child's path to a healthy future is impeded. There are entire fields of psychology centered around this topic, so this is far from a comprehensive overview, but it is important to look at some of what happens when a child is sexualized early.

One of the most unintentionally destructive tendencies we see in a child who has had sexual doors opened in their life, is the unwarranted ownership that they take for the act. When another person, friend, or a family member exposes a child to a sexual act, the child assumes the guilt for what has happened. This so often leads to shame and hiding, which perpetuates the activity, more deeply wounding and sinking the child into this toxic world. These are emotions and desires they were not created to process or control at that age, and therefore unable to handle rightly on their own.

When I was around the age of six our family welcomed into our home a couple and their two young children around my same age who were in need of a place to stay for a month or so. This was, at first, a time of excitement of having new friends to play with and explore the woods surrounding our house but soon led into an experience that would set my life on a spiral that took years to recover from. The older of the two siblings (*who was two years my elder*) began to tell me of how their uncle and their uncle's friend had a game of sorts that they would play with them. Even though I didn't have the language or ability to explain or understand the scope of depravity that my friends had been subjected to, I was told how they had essentially been molested by those two men for an unknown portion of their lives. My new roommate, however, had not only hidden this from their parents, but was continuing to perpetuate this behavior on the younger sibling as well as each new friend that they would meet. This was the beginning of my hiding.

I buried this period deep inside of my memories with a mixture of shame and regret, choosing to cut off a part of my life rather than to face something far too complex and toxic for my heart to handle. The devastation came not only from the opening of those sexual doors in my life and the flood of emotions and desires that followed, but from the guilt and burden of hidden sin that I carried alone for years afterward.

From the age of six and up my family was deeply involved in Rodeo and spent most of our weekends traveling or investing in some sort of horse centered activity, and so we had little time for church. I had a bible, however, that had been given to me as a child and so I would read it often, mostly staying in the gospels, but spending a large portion of time in Proverbs and Ecclesiastes. It was through reading His Word on my own that the Lord began to speak to me and draw my heart to Him to find healing for that ever-present pain from the early loss of innocence. I never told anyone about what had happened to me however, which only served to sink me deeper into a mire of isolation and misidentified pain, leading to more than a dozen years of rebellion, drug abuse, and promiscuity before Jesus stepped in and changed everything.

The goal is to protect our children from exposure to things that damage and steal innocence, but if or when the unthinkable happens, what do we do? We cannot go back into the past to change it, and so we must never waste time in the regret of failure. If a child is sexualized it is imperative to remember that they are not ruined or even damaged goods. You don't have to anticipate rebellion and a life of hidden pain; this only comes when the incident is hidden and left unaddressed. God can and will use everything for good! In Jesus, woundings become opportunities and launchpads into greater realms than otherwise would have been possible. This is never to justify something terrible, but rather to exalt the incredible power of God to weave every aspect of our lives (*good as well as bad*) into a tapestry of His will and glory that is far too great for us to comprehend in this life. When a horrible event is handed to our Father, He will make something glorious out of it!

It is crucial to have good, open communication with a child who has had sexual doors opened in their life. Let them know that although it was wrong, and even though they may have participated in it, it is not their burden to carry, and the Lord can wash them clean from all of it. This is a beautiful opportunity to lead them into healing by showing them *the two sides of forgiveness.*

The first side of forgiveness is receiving it from the Lord. Talk to them about sin and how every single one of us has fallen into it, and all of us need to be forgiven. They know that their participation in the act was not right because they already feel shame for it, and so this is the perfect time to lead them to talk to Jesus and ask His forgiveness, assuring them that He will completely forgive and make them pure. The next side of forgiveness is forgiving the person who led them into it. This is essential, as the Lord tells us in Mathew 6:14-15 that, *"if you forgive others their sin the Father will also forgive you, but if you do not forgive them their sin, neither will the Father forgive you."* Walk them through the truth that forgiving someone doesn't mean that their action was ok, but instead it releases us from the poison of what they did to us and opens our hearts to receive forgiveness from the Father. When we turn to the Father, confess our sins, and repent He always completely forgives us and cleanses us from all unrighteousness (*1 John 1:9*). This is the first part of healing that we must lead into.

Good, healthy community, diligent oversight, and regular check-ins with the child are the essential next steps as you navigate their way through continued healing. This, coupled with a deepening relationship with them centered around Jesus, will lead them into restoration of innocence and a course correction back onto the path of life. Remember, as damaging as early sexualization is, much more damage is done through shame and hiding, both of which are eliminated by early recognition of the act and intentionally leading the child to the feet of our Father.

WARNING SIGNS

Whenever these types of issues begin to occur, don't ignore or excuse them. It doesn't always mean that a sexual door has been opened, but in every case these signs warrant you patiently drawing your child closer in relationship to determine what truly is the cause of their behavior.

- Mood swings (*depression, anxiety, unable to get out of bed in the morning…*)

- Becoming disinterested in the activities and things they previously enjoyed

- Harmful to animals or people smaller than them

- Harmful to themselves

- Emotional outbursts (*unwarranted over sensitivity to situations*)

- Extreme personality deviations

- Nightmares

- Running away

- Unaccountable fear of people or places

- Regressive behaviors (*bed wetting, crying unnecessarily, thumb sucking...*)

- Withdrawing from relationship with family

Have conversations with your child. Don't give into the spirit of suspicion, but use discernment. Sometimes all we have to go on is a parent's intuition which must be taken to the Lord for His voice and input on the matter. He will guide us into the answer!

PART 5

Launching

NAVIGATING RISK

Imagine a fifteen-month-old child playing in the living room. This child can walk on his own now and is beginning to explore more courageously as he learns lessons of balance and gravity. Say in this scenario, there is a split-level living room with one step, giving about an eight-to-ten-inch drop from one level to the other.

As you are watching this child play on the upper level, you notice that he is getting closer and closer to the tiny precipice, and you begin to foresee the coming micro-calamity. In your previous experience you have seen the child fall, bump his head and cry – a situation that slightly broke your heart and caused you to desire to prevent that type of unnecessary pain from happening again.

Now, you have a choice to make. Do you tell him not to play on the step, causing possible defiance, tears, or the need to monitor for a while to make sure the rule is followed? Do you walk over and pick the child up and place him on the lower level, thereby avoiding a mini scene, tears, and the need to take time to console him through the coming fall? Do you sit closely by, pretending not to watch, and then quickly reach out and catch him as soon as his foot slips over the edge? Or do you just watch and see what happens?

Any of these answers can be correct, depending on his age and experience, especially if you apply them in that order, but not any one of them will work on their own forever. Sooner or later the child is going to need to understand and experience how to navigate these challenges of life, and keeping him from the problem will not solve the problem. So often we as parents, in our righteous desire to keep our children from hurt or harm, end up injuring the child by over-shielding them from minimal and necessary consequences which allow them to learn and navigate the challenges of life.

Experience is necessary but timing is crucial. If this were a four-month-old child, the effort in trying to teach them to maneuver down even a single stair would be wasted. Gauging the child's age and ability to receive and process the information is important in determining their success.

As parents we are called to shelter our children from the damaging aspects of the world, while simultaneously preparing them to be masters over it. If a child is protected from the harm of an obstacle without being taught how to safely traverse it, they will grow up with the needless disability of believing they must always avoid that obstacle, or be reliant on another to do what they ultimately should be able to do themselves. Our children will be those who approach life with thoughtful courage!

THE ART OF REASON

Have you ever met someone who just seems to deal well with situations they find themselves in? Somebody who has the ability to assess a scenario and call it for what it is? There is something so refreshing about a person who can see the world around them clearly and confidently, yet lovingly, respond rightly to it. This is not only who we want to be, but also the kind of person that we want our kids to be.

Philippians 4:5 tells us to, *"Let your reasonableness be known to everyone."* In order to let our reasonableness be known to others, we must first be reasonable. This means that we must possess the ability to not only reason, but also be a person who can be reasoned with.

As my daughters were growing up, I remember they would often ask me a particular question whenever we were discussing different current events or issues we saw in our society; why would someone do that?

One day as we were driving to church one of them asked me why someone who was addicted to meth would sell all they had to continue doing something that was slowly killing them. *"Don't they know that the drugs are poison?"* They asked? My answer would always come back to this; *sin is not reasonable.* You can't bring rational thoughts to try to convince a person out of sin, because sin isn't a matter of intellectual miseducation, it is a spiritual deception.

This is how fear is. Have you ever tried to reason with someone who is having a panic attack? *"Settle down. There is nothing here that can hurt you, so you, therefore, are now not afraid..."* It just doesn't work! We do have a choice on whether or not we will decide to be afraid, but once engaged in fearfulness our brain stops listening to rationale. Fear is a spiritual decision to back away from the Father and believe the enemy.

When I speak of fear, I'm not referring to the rarest of occasions such as seeing your child standing on the edge of a cliff, but rather everyday situations. There are myriads of times when our child is doing something that isn't quite dangerous, but still sends a little shockwave of anxiety down a parent's neck as they watch, increasing the desire to make a snap decision.

There do exist times when a quick reaction

must be made to save a child from danger, but the vast majority of situations allow time for us as parents to think and consider the options. What are the possible negative consequences if I allow my child to climb that tree, or hike in the woods behind our house, or catch a non-venomous snake? Am I just projecting my personal fears, or am I using reason to truly discern if there is danger? What really are the chances for a life changing consequence to happen my child? Using reason to accurately read a situation will eliminate wasted time on unnecessary boundaries and allow the child to explore the world so they can learn without fear.

I grew up with an unquenchable fascination with wildlife, especially wildlife that I could catch and examine close up, and one of the most easily obtainable animals for me were snakes. My parents taught me early on the difference between the venomous and non-venomous species, which was easy since the only venomous snake around was the rattlesnake; all others were fair game. I quickly learned that a bite from a bull-snake, rat-snake, garter-snake, or a yellowbellied racer only resulted in a pinch and was nothing to fear. When I had friends who came to visit, however, their only experience with snakes was mostly movies about deadly, poisonous serpents who wrought havoc on society. It usually took a while to convince them of the harmlessness of these beautiful creatures.

One day when a cousin came up to visit, I immediately brought out and showed her my latest acquisition, a large three-foot bull snake. She had heard stories from our uncle in Africa of dangerous cobras and black mambas, and this snake was no different in her mind. Her response was to cringe and threaten that any sudden moves would be met with disastrous consequences to me personally, as I laughed and assured her that this was just a bull-snake and actually quite harmless.

As those words left my mouth the snake suddenly drew up and snapped out, latching its jaws firmly on my arm. I yelled out of surprise, and then laughed, which did nothing to calm my cousin's uncontrolled panic and subsequent flight out of the house. I shook loose the snake's grip from my forearm and put it back in its terrarium, but the damage was done; my cousin would never again believe a word I said about snakes, neither would she ever again set foot in a house that was home to one. The bull-snake bite was neither venomous nor painful, and so her fear was completely irrational, but how do you explain that to someone fleeing for their life?

Isn't this a common way that we as parents respond to a situation that makes us uncomfortable? We see something that is scary to us personally, and rather than clearly looking at what the danger is (*or isn't*), we make the judgement based on our own fears, preconceived notions, and previous interactions with it. Our children will eventually react to situations in the same way that we do, with either irrationality or calm reason. I have many pictures and memories of my four-and-five-year-old daughters with huge smiles, catching and holding snakes longer than they were tall. My kids don't go snake hunting like I did as a child, but they have no irrational fears for them.

Look at the situation. What is the likelihood of a negative outcome? What is the worst that would come of that consequence? In the case of the bull-snake, there was a mid-level possibility of me being bitten, but the consequence was extremely minimal and resulted in a small pinch, but then laughter and better reflexes for the next time.

When the negative consequences are *minimal,* don't waste time forbidding the event, as it will most likely result in fun and learning. When negative consequences are *detrimental,* take the possibility into account. If the possibility is extremely low, then maybe add some extra precautions and oversight, but don't waste time forbidding it.

A meteor landing on someone is devastating, but extremely rare. A cougar attack could be life changing but chances of that happening are about one in a billion, so go hiking, and *don't change plans based on tiny possibilities of negative outcomes.* Be bold and courageous and teach your children to be the same!

Reason doesn't ever override the Holy Spirit's voice in the moment, as there are times when He tells us to choose a path that is completely contrary to our own understanding. Listening to and seeking His direction is paramount, but so often He is asking us to use the sound mind (*2 Timothy 1:7*) which He has given us to navigate the situation.

Reasoning allows for sound patterns of decision-making skills to be established, which will foster soil that grows wisdom, courage and ultimately a well-rounded man or woman. The idea behind embracing reason is to evaluate the situation that your child is in through an objective and realistic lens, so that we as parents can encourage adventure, confidence, and growth. It is essential to recognize our own fears as a parent so that we can deal rightly with them in a way that will prevent passing them on to the next generation. All negative cycles and generational curses must stop with us, and we must resolve to do whatever it takes to make our ceiling the floor for our children to build upon!

LAUNCH PAD INTO ADULTHOOD

Our whole purpose as parents is to raise children to be healthy, responsible adults who love and follow God. How often is a child seen as their parent's emotional support, reason for living, marriage anchor, or just their little buddy? A child's heart is not designed to carry the weight of any of those roles. So often a grown man is still seen as their momma's little baby boy, or a grown woman still treated as daddy's little princess. This is not to diminish the deepest place of love that a child will forever hold in the heart of their parent, but it is to highlight the so often misunderstood or abused role that the parent is entrusted by God to fulfill; to train and raise the child to be a strong, independent man or woman of God.

As the child grows, the relationship shifts. A teenager no longer needs to have their diapers changed and their clothes picked out for them.

They now need a parent who will have difficult and sometimes awkward conversations about what they are experiencing in life at their age. A toddler may need to be consoled when they stub their toe, whereas a twelve-year-old needs to be led to endure that physical pain. The relationship changes in regard to how we interact with them and what information we decide they are mature enough to handle, but our goal of raising them to be an adult never does.

We must enjoy and embrace every stage of life that our child is in, because every stage is truly better than the last! It is natural to look back with nostalgia on earlier times, but if you are stuck missing and romanticizing the times when your child was younger, then be assured that you are currently missing the time they are in now! Missing the moment the child is currently in will ultimately result in future regret for not having been fully engaged in it.

Continue to grow as a parent and allow the relationship to evolve as you do. Few relationships are as fulfilling as a grown parent with their grown kids, while few are as damaging and toxic as a parent still clinging to and treating their adult son or daughter as they did when they were a child.

EVER GROWING BOUNDARIES

When it comes to boundaries, there is a ditch on each side of the path of life. The ditch we find on one side is tyranny with over-regulated control, while the other side is rebellion surrounded by chaos. The middle of the path of life, however, is freedom coupled with obedience. The Father gave us a blueprint for this in the Garden of Eden.

After the Lord created Adam, He gave him an abundance of freedom with only one rule; *do not eat from the tree of the knowledge of good and evil*. Notice that the Lord didn't give lists of rules surrounding all of the other freedoms, or safety nets which would prevent Adam from exploring, just a rule that would protect him from the danger of death. The question of why the Lord even put that tree in the garden is one about which entire books can be written on, and so we won't delve too deeply into it for now, but there is a lesson we can draw out of it that directly applies to this topic. *Without the option for disobedience, there is no ability to walk in true obedience.* There can be no true love without the option to choose not to love. The Lord is showing us that freedom is essential, but obedience is crucial.

God didn't put us on the earth so we could just live in a beautiful paradise at our own leisure, and our purpose as parents must reflect this mindset. While making a safe, loving home for our children is of great importance, as parents our goal must never be solely to make a perfect paradise for them to live in. Yes, we are called to love them, but loving them also looks like challenging their limitations, training their minds, and testing their obedience. It doesn't have to look like a military training camp though; it is actually something we can step into through fun and adventure together!

There was once a study done involving people who took their dogs to two different dog parks: one with a fence and one without. The dogs who were set free inside of the fenced park ran all around the perimeter and enjoyed the park freely, while those who were released in the park without fences were timid and reluctant to venture too far from their masters.

The correlation relates directly to the

amount of security that good boundaries provide for children. The smaller the child, the greater the need for tighter boundaries and environmental assurance. For example, a baby needs to be fed, carried, comforted, have their diapers changed, and kept warm or cool in order to survive. Basically every aspect of their life is dependent on extremely tight boundaries and control. Even the simplest of choices must be made for them.

A toddler, however, is capable of feeding and dressing themselves to some extent, while still needing their food and clothes provided and sometimes chosen for them. If a teenager is still needing their mother to choose their food and clothing for them, then there is a major issue. These are some very obvious examples, but this principle also applies to less apparent areas that, if aren't allowed to develop healthily, will lead to a child who eventually blows past unnecessary and restrictive boundaries without permission.

When our daughters were young, we decided they wouldn't taste sugary food until their first piece of cake on their one-year birthday. What lead to this decision was simply that sugar is extremely unhealthy for a child, and they will eat anything you feed them, so why not make it healthy? Once a child gets a taste for sugar, look out!

Not long after Ruth's third birthday (*and her*

further experience with cake), I was on my way home from work and decided to stop off at the store and pick up some donuts. When I brought them inside, I mentioned to Folake how I had picked up some cake donuts. This grabbed Ruth's attention right away, and her eyes locked onto the box I was carrying. She asked if she could have one, but wanting to keep her from the knowledge of yet another source of sugar, I declined her request.

That night, at around two in the morning, I woke up and walked to the kitchen to grab a glass of water. As I rounded the corner, I saw a scene that will forever live in my mind. There was Ruth standing on a chair, a donut in each hand, and cheeks bulging with the last remaining donut from the box. This moment was so hilarious, and so out of character for Ruth that all I could do was hug her and laugh as I took her back to her bed. I recognized my folly in trying to keep her out of the world of donuts, and the next day expanded her boundaries to include eating this delicious treat with her dad.

The more a child grows, the more the boundaries must grow with them. This is not only healthy but extremely necessary! It is common for a parent to begin to find worth and identity in the need that their son or daughter has for them while still young. As the child grows and the need lessens, the parent can sometimes begin to feel insecure, as if a part of their identity is slipping away. Unfortunately, this can sometimes cause the parent to find unhealthy ways to continue to foster their child's dependency on them, thereby stunting the growth of the child and preventing them from developing the skills necessary to step into well rounded adulthood.

It is essential for us as parents to not only set boundaries for our children that grow with them, but in doing so to also *create boundaries for ourselves in relationship to them*. There are ways we as parents once operated which worked well in that season of life, but now must be set aside to make room for new methods which require a higher level of maturity and discipline in ourselves.

These are times when we must be willing give up more and more of the previous functions we once performed in our child's life and exchange them for more hands-off roles. This allows us to then encourage our child to step into their next level of maturity by taking on areas of their life which are no longer necessary for us as parents to carry.

Soon there will come a day when your son or daughter no longer needs your boundaries. By this time, the boundaries should have grown so broad and be so well known as to not even have the need to be enforced. The goal by that day is for our children to have replaced our boundaries with those they find in their relationship with God.

This is the incredible transition our children must make from seeing you (*their parent*) as the boundary maker, to finding that quality in their true Father, God. When this transition is made, the son or daughter will receive the Lord's Word and His Spirit as the ultimate guide and boundary for their lives. *This is our goal!*

This illustrates why it is so imperative that we spend our lives investing into our child's character so when the time comes when we are no longer needed to carry the responsibility of choice in their lives, we can trust that they already have everything necessary to succeed by making the right decisions. This takes intentionality and self-control on our part to turn off our *"parenting autopilot,"* and to grow and seek the Lord on what the next phase of parenting looks like, for both our child as well as for ourselves.

AFTERWORD

This book is intended not only to speak wisdom into the raising of the next generation, but to give insight into the ways that each of us have individually been raised, in order to recognize how it has manifested in our own lives as adults. Correctly perceiving the root reasons for some of our current behaviors allows us to go back with the Father to those original moments to find healing and redemption, ultimately receiving His Fathering in the deepest places of our hearts.

The most important and impactful thing any parent can do in the life of their child is to continuously seek and grow closer to the Lord. Children follow where we go, not where we tell them to go. *Your effectiveness as a parent will only be as powerful as your relationship with the Father.* Seek Him!

I think it is also worth saying that every part of this book is impossible to do on our own. Without a deepening walk with the Lord, all of these principles will just be markers and reminders of areas in our lives that we can't live up to. On the other hand, when we ask the Holy Spirit to fill us with His grace and empower us to walk in step with Him we will receive the ability to live this out at a greater capacity and on a higher level than is even written in this book.

These writings only highlight the places we must bring to the Lord so that His power can operate in us and turn our lives into words which will speak down through generations long after we are gone. Only by walking in step with Him can we have an impact that will continue into eternity.

Children, both spiritual as well as physical, are the most precious and priceless things that exist in all of creation! Cover them in prayer, asking the Lord for His hand upon them, because ultimately, not only does He love them more extravagantly and abundantly than we ever could, but His favor and protection over them is far more comprehensive and desirable than our plan for their lives could ever be. The Lord has them in His hands. Trust Him and make the most of this time He has given you by showing them how to love and walk with Jesus.

BOOKSBYROSS.COM

Checkout these other books by Ross Kellogg

Close Conflict

Close Conflict Expanded Edition

Made in the USA
Columbia, SC
15 February 2025